SELLING LEASING
IN A TOUGH ECONOMY

For information, contact:

ExecutiveCaliber—Global Lease Training
2144 South 1150 East
Bountiful, UT 84010

First edition

United States Cataloguing in Publications Data

Taylor, Jeffrey
Selling Leasing in a Tough Economy

0-9727047-0-1

1. Taylor, Jeffrey
2. Leasing
3. Selling
4. Title

LEASING.BZ

For Purchases, contact:
Jeffrey Taylor, CLP
ExecutiveCaliber—Global Lease Training
2144 South 1150 East
Bountiful, UT 84010 USA
(801) 299-9332
(801) 299-9932 (fax)

To Toby, my wife, lover and friend

"She didn't mean to be sexy that moment, but even a winter nightgown couldn't hide that lovely outline. When will I outgrow my simple-minded fascination with the form she had happened to choose for her body? Never, I thought."

-Richard David Bach,
US author, Jonathan Livingston Seagull

ACKNOWLEDGMENTS

I would like to thank the following people who guided me in the development of this book:

Ellen Singer, editor, who promised and delivered pristine copyediting while guiding me through the complex and mysterious world of publishing.

Marie LeTourneau, illustrator, who clearly demonstrated in her portfolio that her classic training would uniquely qualify her to create images of distinction.

Khalid Rizwan, technical guru, who worked endless hours to deliver an easy-to-use, on-line HTML order form that not only works but is beautiful in its simplicity.

Nilay Chatterjee, logo designer, who created a multi-colored logo which truly reflects the global movement of equipment leasing.

Ron Pramschufer, of RJ Communications, and Steve Ebenger, of Bang Printing, for taking a complex PDF file and giving it life.

Jonathan Gullery of Budget Book Design for stepping in at the last moment and saving the day.

And to the following list of equipment leasing veterans, who taught me how to be humble in the midst of turmoil:

Sudhir Amembal
Sue Angelucci
Bill Bosco
Joe Cannon
Ron Caruso
Neal Fishman
Steven Geller, CLP
Ken Goodman, CLP
Jon S. Haas, CLP
Shawn Halladay
Rod Hurd
David G. Mayer
John McCue
Kit Menkin
Lisa Rafter

Contents

INTRODUCTION

I have worked continually with the equipment leasing industry since 1981 and, as a result, become an expert. I have loved every moment of my career educating thousands of leasing professionals all over the world. Now, more than ever, education is crucial, because many leasing professionals are unprepared for the rough economic times ahead.

I have observed too many leasing professionals who lose sales due to lack of knowledge, bad behavior, marketing to the wrong people, saying dumb things, and not doing their homework.

It is through this book that I hope to correct this problem.

If you have not obtained wealth in this industry, you have to first stop blaming everyone around you and, second, analyze everything you hear, say and do.

If you're like me – and most people – you take no joy in looking at yourself and grading your performance. The task is difficult, painful and intrusive. But the only way to get to a new horizon is to figure out where you are now and chart your own unique future. Unfortunately, there is no way to obtain success without a lot of hard work, time and effort.

I believe that with proper guidance and education, everyone can become financially successful in the leasing industry.

Allow me the opportunity to open your mind to new ideas and let me guide you on your leasing journey.

Chapter 1

WELCOME TO THE EQUIPMENT LEASING INDUSTRY

So you want to sell leases for a living?

Let me ask you something:

Are you prepared for the tough times ahead? Are you ready to join an industry that's in trouble and under attack by accountants, tax professionals, the US government, SEC, IASB and the world community? Do you want to associate yourself with Enron, GE, Tyco and Global Crossing?

Before you respond, let me continue:

Are you ready to battle every single day with other superstars? Are you prepared to starve until you make your first big sale? Can you afford to wait 3-6 months before you see a commission check? Can you see yourself selling a product that has been labeled by the press as "smoke and mirrors"?

Let me give you some advice. I've been consulting to the leasing industry for more than twenty years. I've seen the good years and I've seen the bad. Believe me, things are going to get worse before they get better. Why? Because there are thousands of lessors chasing too few deals and not enough good credits to go around. Some lessors will eventually give up, shut their doors and sell their existing deals for cash to pay off their creditors.

How do I know that this is the future? Let me go back to 1961.

I'm 10 years old. My father is an arbitrageur in New York City. He commutes on the Erie Lackawanna from Livingston, New Jersey to Hoboken and then takes the tube to Wall Street. He returns every evening on the 6:02 PM and walks through the front door at 7:00 PM. Mom readies dinner as we all sit down to eat, just like Ozzie & Harriet or Father Knows Best. Dad tells us about his trades and how much money he made that day. He recalls in minute detail how he took advantage of the other side. In other words, he recalls in vivid color how he killed the enemy.

I did not really understand what was going on. I was too young to comprehend not only what he did but how he did it. On top of that, I was afraid to ask questions or say anything because I felt intimidated.

At the end of the week, on Saturday, he would take me with him to his office on the 37th floor of the Chase Manhattan Plaza. I looked forward to being with him, because it was only him and me. I had Dad to myself.

I got to ride the train and look out the window with youthful amazement as the countryside passed by with alarming speed. At the end of the line, the conductor would flip the green and brown reversible seat backs, pick up the punched tickets and prepare the train for the next trip.

Unfortunately, I did not dare say a word because Dad was engrossed in his research papers. I remember the green and white IBM forms which he would flip through and doggy ear to make sure that he knew what his next move was going to be. He always smiled when he knew what he was going to do.

Dad's team met every Saturday at 9:00 AM and would work through lunch, which was always catered. It felt religious to discuss, analyze what they did right and wrong, and how they were going to revamp their game plan for the next week. I eavesdropped on their animated conversations while I copied position papers for Dad on the office's Bruning machine, a chemical-based toning process that preceded the modern day Xerox.

He would tell me that, when I was older, there would be a guaranteed place for me on the trading desk. He would show me the 'turret' and explain that if you pushed this button you got the floor of the stock exchange. A second button would connect him with another brokerage firm. A third button would connect him with Europe and so on. He would tell me how much money all the traders made and that I should appreciate the opportunity that was awaiting me. He felt good that he could not only plan my fate but hand it to me on a silver platter.

Dad loved Wall Street. He said it was the only industry that could make you money regardless of whether the client bought or sold. Didn't matter. If you were lucky enough to work there, you made money on each and every trade. Even if the client lost everything.

As a kid, it seemed like fantasy land. One problem, though. Everyone always referred to me as Howie's kid. Never Jeffrey. And I hated that. So I vowed that I would never work on Wall Street. I wanted to be my own person and have the market recognize me for my own talents.

I think Dad never forgave me for going into leasing. I'll never know since he had a stroke and doesn't recognize much of anything now. There are times that I think he caused his own problems; he refused to take his doctor-prescribed blood pressure medication. Dad thought he knew more than anyone else, including God, and went out in the hot Florida sun to play a rigorous round of tennis. Although he was in great shape for 64, he tempted fate once too often. The neurosurgeon gave him three months to live. And that was eleven years ago.

As it would turn out, I became a CPA and wound up with a Big 8 firm. Since Dad was a CPA and Grandpa Charlie was a CPA, it made a lot of sense. Nonetheless, I failed the exam two times before I finally passed it after two-and-a-half years. I would like to think that the passing of the exam, as brutal as it was, opened doors for me. In 1981, as the US government was reeling under 21 percent interest rates, I got my first leasing break.

At the time, I was living in San Francisco (I got transferred there by Citibank to work for their foreign exchange operations — I quit when they tried to send me back to New York) and working for Peat Marwick's consulting group. There was a bank in Seattle, called SeaFirst Bank, who had a leasing division that could not get a clean audit from Arthur Andersen. SeaFirst hated AA and wanted another CPA firm to come in and help them clean up their operations. Their accounting systems

were in disarray and no one could prove the numbers. The only problem — no one
on the auditing side knew COBOL. And I did.

Over the years, I combined my COBOL and CPA skills to fix systems for all of
Peat's major leasing clients — GE, Barclays, GATX, New England Merchant Leasing,
Security Pacific, BankAmerica and First Union, to name a few. I lived on the road
and learned everything I could about how all leasing departments worked.

While I learned the business and began to see how all of the pieces fit together,
I got to meet some of the industry's best sales people. I listened to every word of
advice that I was fortunate to receive and started to keep journals of ideas, methods,
and tricks of the trade.

I developed a reputation for getting the job done and on time. I was treated
well and started to make a lot of money. I traveled extensively, was never home
and moved from San Francisco to North Carolina to personally manage two of Peat's
southeastern clients.

One day, in 1984, I browsed the local newsstand and fixated on a magazine
called Entrepreneur. It was their first edition and I threw my entire accounting career
away to develop my first PC-based training business (The Leasing Coach). I mortgaged
the house with a 2nd, made a lot of money for a couple of years, misread the market
in 1987, and lost all of my material assets and marriage in the process.

I moved back to New York and lived in Dad's corporate apartment in the city.
He lectured me on not listening to him and living too well. He said I needed to suffer
more and decided to side with my ex-wife for abandoning her by being on the road
too much. He helped her draft the divorce agreement and forced me into financial
and emotional bankruptcy.

Years went by as I tried to get my life back on track. I took on consulting jobs,
but the cash flow was unpredictable and uneven. There were many times when I
didn't even know how I could pay Dad the rent. .At one point, I was in a sleazy
run-down hotel in Minneapolis and I seriously considered killing myself. I called Dad
for advice and he told me to stop feeling sorry for myself, wired me $50 and told
me to go out for a nice dinner.

Several years later I was still single in NYC. I hung around the singles clubs and got to meet graduate students from the University of Chicago. I would play tennis in Long Island City and play piano for tips at the local bars. It is not as glamorous as Billy Joel makes you want to believe.

Having nothing to lose, I take an American Express financed vacation to Club Med in Turk & Caicos, a small Caribbean island near Cuba. I met Toby, with whom I immediately fall in love. She doesn't believe me when I tell her this. She thinks that I am confusing love with sex. Ten days later, back in NYC, I played for her an original song that I composed on the only furniture left over from my divorce; an 1898, seven-and-half-foot Concert Grand Beckstein piano, handmade in Berlin.

I continued to find consulting projects. I tracked down one of my old friends, John McCue, who told me that if I can afford to get to the annual ELA conference, he will allow me to work in his booth.

Upon discovery of my presence in John's booth, ELA attendees tell John that he is violating ELA rules, which prevent more than one vendor in a booth. John defended me and put his career on the line. To this day, I still owe him for that beautiful gift of compassion.

As it would pass, I got to meet Sudhir Amembal, the founder of the lease training industry. Sudhir told me that he is expanding his business and that he thinks I would be great as a full-time classroom instructor. For two years he flew Toby and me to his home state of Utah for skiing. If his intent was to show me how much fun I could have in Utah, it worked; still I remained skeptical about the idea of becoming a teacher and reluctant to give up New York.

By 1995, Toby and I were living in Putnam County, 100 miles north of NYC, and New York entered a prolonged recession. Sudhir's offer began to look attractive. We were tempted but nervous. We looked at our alternatives and decided to give up New York and move to Salt Lake City, Utah.

I worked for Sudhir, Shawn Halladay and John Deane for five years. In return for writing material for senior management and other instructors, developing new courses, running leasing conferences and creating PC-based software models, they agreed to teach me the lease training business.

One year later, by surprise, Sudhir and team sold out to Euromoney, a British conglomerate, for millions. I decided to stay with Euromoney on the condition that they agree to let Toby and me stay in Utah. All of the other instructors quit, left the industry or started competitive firms.

Five years later, after rebuilding the business, Euromoney informed me they no longer needed my services. They told me that I became too expensive and that they could not afford me anymore.

Toby and I talked that night for hours. My kids were still living with my ex-wife in North Carolina and Toby's children worked back in New York. We questioned our next move. Should we stay in Utah? Should I stay in lease training? Should we move back to New York? Decisions had to be made fast. We were quickly running out of choices.

We agreed that we would stay in Utah and that I would develop my own business. Toby argued that I should be able to succeed – I had the experience in North Carolina. I conceded that I may not have another opportunity – I was by then 50. We determine that if we cut down on expenses (i.e. cut out entertainment and eating out) we can get by for six-nine months.

Soon after, I built my first website, http://executivecaliber.ws. I picked up a HTML book and learned how to code text, graphics and audio. I traveled to San Francisco to a search engine conference and figured out how to get listed in the top ten for "lease training" at Yahoo, Google, Lycos, AltaVista and other major search engines.

I worked day and night, never saw Toby and slept downstairs due to my irregular hours. I worked every day on building a website, dreaming that one day I would be seen by every leasing professional who is looking for lease training.

Weeks passed and the telephone didn't ring. I started advertising in the Molloy Monitor. I saw people hitting on my website but received no phone calls.

I started a free weekly leasing newsletter, called Lease Accounting, Tax and Politics using an e-newsletter company called Constant Contact. After weeks of spidering leasing websites, I developed a list of 3000 leasing e-mail addresses. I pitched them my free newsletter and told them about my free lease training website.

One day, I got a phone call from a gentleman who told me that he met me, a year ago, at a Euromoney conference. He wants me to come out to California to help his sales team improve their performance.

I then got a call from a regional bank in Indiana who also wants sales training. After that, I received the opportunity to work with a global captive finance company in Canada.

After nine months of developing and fine-tuning my mailing lists, I reached 11,000 readers in 75 countries and begin to lecture internationally in Italy, Malta, Australia and Singapore. After 18 months, I reached 13,000 readers in 110 countries. Search engines have discovered me for keyword searches "lease training", "FASB 13" and "leadership" and usually rank one or more of my websites in the top three on page 1.

Later on I added more websites to house material I wrote twenty years ago (leasecoach.com) and started a leasing academy for advanced sales training (leasingacademy.com).

Finally, after months and months of searching I landed the rights to the website, leasing.bz, which is my promotional website for this book.

The primary purpose for me sharing with you these travails is simple. I want to:

- *Share with you my own experiences*
- *Show you that it is possible to succeed with impossible odds*
- *Guide you to be the best person you can be*
- *Help you improve your own selling capabilities*

Welcome to the leasing industry!

Chapter 2

WILL LEASING SURVIVE?

Leasing is corporate America's biggest source of equipment finance. It's bigger than bank loans, bonds, stocks, and commercial mortgages. In 2001, over $240 billion dollars of equipment was leased in the United States and $473 billion dollars throughout the world. Overall, worldwide leasing volume continues to grow. Unfortunately, volumes in several countries have dropped precipitously due to the worldwide slowdown.

U.S. companies lease everything from printing presses to power plants, hay balers to helicopters, office copiers to offshore drilling rigs, telecom equipment to large-scale computer networks.

Over 35 percent of all capital equipment is financed through some form of leasing. Eight out of ten companies - from mom and pop proprietorships to the Fortune 500 — turn to leasing to get ahead and stay ahead.

How did we get here? How did leasing become the most popular financing alternative in the world? Let's explore its rich history.

In 1984, while the leasing industry was reeling from the third major tax change in four years, archaeologists found clay tablets from the ancient Samarian city of Ur, documenting farm equipment leases from the year 2010 B.C.

Fifty years later, the king of Babylonia in his famous Code of Hammurabi enacted the first leasing laws. The ancient civilizations of Egypt, Greece and Rome engaged in leasing transactions of real and personal property, while the Phoenicians actively promoted leasing by chartering ships to local merchants.

Leasing first appeared in the United States in the 1700s to finance the use of horse-drawn wagons. By the mid-1800s, railroad tycoons, battling to extend their private railroads across the country, required tremendous amounts of new capital. Most banks, however, considered railroad financing risky and refused to lend to the emerging transportation industry. Locomotives, cars and other railroad equipment had to be financed using new and creative methods - the forerunners of the equipment lease.

This new scheme involved third-party investors who would pool their funds, purchase railroad cars from a manufacturer, then lease the cars to the railroad in the form of "equipment trust certificates". The railroad would receive title to the equipment after making periodic payments to cover the purchase price plus interest costs assessed by the lender. This method of financing resembles the modern-day conditional sale.

In the early 1900s, companies began to act as lessors for equipment by leasing it out while maintaining title to it. Often, the lessees would be shippers who wanted control over their shipments without the responsibilities of ownership. This method introduced the operating or true lease concept. Meanwhile, other manufacturers were looking for additional ways to sell their merchandise. They created the installment sale, which allowed commercial markets to increase their purchasing power by paying for equipment over time.

By the mid-1920s, manufacturers were basing too many major investment decisions on credit sales. Their failure to recognize this danger helped bring about the Great Depression in the 1930s. As many businesses suffered, they became wary of "creative" financing, and leasing was placed on hold.

Leasing returned to popularity during World War II. Manufacturers entered into cost-plus contracts with the government. These contracts allowed the manufacturer to recover actual costs plus a guaranteed profit. In order to minimize costs, many of these companies leased special-purpose machinery from the government. Companies discovered that they could return the equipment to the government at the end of the lease thus protecting themselves against owning technically obsolete equipment when the war ended.

In the 1950s, consumers started to demand a vast array of goods. They wanted speed, convenience and mobility. Manufacturers turned to leasing to help them quickly overhaul old operations and to create modern facilities for the production of new products such as televisions, advanced communications equipment and airplanes.

This rapid growth provided an ideal backdrop for the creation of a formal equipment leasing industry.

In spite of a strong US dollar, volatile exchange rates and unpredictable interest rates, the leasing industry continues to survive and expand. Currently, there is worldwide competition to serve lessees among banks, insurance companies, captive finance companies, third-party vendors, brokers, and independent leasing companies. What were the major factors that helped make leasing the popular financial alternative that it is today?

The volatility of the general economy was one factor. Leasing, once considered to be aggressive financing used only by those unable to get conventional terms, is now regarded as a stable alternative to wildly-fluctuating interest and inflation rates. For example:

- *In December 1980, the prime lending rate reached 21.5 percent and low-risk instruments like U.S. Treasury bonds stood at 17 percent.*
- *Double-digit inflation became common in the 1970s, causing many assets to be priced out of reach without financing.*
- *Annual federal budget deficits climbed continuously, from $25 billion in 1968 to a staggering $230 billion in 1990, causing the national debt to reach a mind-boggling $2.7 trillion.*

This financial roller coaster caused many traditional funding sources to tighten their credit requirements, opening the door to new methods. At the same time favorable tax laws and other regulations bolstered leasing.

Let's return to the 1950s to see why some of these favorable changes were brought about.

In 1953, with the nation in a post-war slump, Congress wanted to promote capital formation and manufacturing. In response, the IRS issued the Internal Revenue Code of 1954. Section 167 of that code gave the equipment's owner/lessor the ability to (1) deduct ordinary expenses associated with a lease and (2) accelerate depreciation by using either the 200 percent declining balance or the sum-of-the-years digits method.

By increasing tax deductions in the early life of the asset and deferring taxable income to the later years, the Code was intended to enhance the benefits of ownership and encourage capital spending. However, many companies, such as railroads and airlines, couldn't afford the outright purchase of the costly equipment they needed to operate. For these companies, the new tax benefits were meaningless.

U.S. Leasing Corporation was the first general equipment leasing company formed to take advantage of these tax benefits of ownership while passing the right to use the equipment and the expense of maintenance to another party. In these transactions, title usually passed to lessees upon their exercise of a nominal purchase option.

By 1955 the use of leasing had spread, and several more leasing companies entered the market. While they were bringing new products into the leasing arena at a rapid rate, a major tax issue was surfacing. The tax code, which had been issued by the IRS the previous year, had not distinguished clearly between a true lease and a conditional sale agreement. Since leasing companies didn't want to lose any of these newfound tax benefits, they were reluctant to pursue deals that might be questioned by the IRS.

With the intention of defining a true lease for tax purposes, the IRS issued Revenue Ruling 55-540 in 1955. This ruling classified a transaction as a true lease only if none of the following conditions was true:

1. *Any portion of the lease payments was applied to an equity position in the asset*
2. *Ownership automatically passed to the lessee at the end of the term*

3. The amount paid under a short-term lease was a significant portion of the purchase price
4. Rental payments were substantially higher than fair market
5. The transaction contained a nominal purchase option
6. Any portion of the lease payment was characterized as interest

If any one of these conditions was true, the transaction was considered a conditional sale, and only the lessee received the tax benefits.

During the remainder of the 1950s, the economy remained somewhat flat. A mild recession in 1960-61 once again spurred Congress to action, resulting in dramatic changes in the leasing industry.

In another effort to pump up capital expenditures, Congress introduced in 1962 a new tax benefit, which would provide the leasing industry with its biggest boost to date. The Investment Tax Credit (ITC) provided purchasers of capital equipment with a tax credit they could use to offset their total tax liability to the government. The purchaser could determine the amount of this credit by taking 7 percent of the original equipment cost.

Lessors who could establish true leases were also entitled to the ITC. Therefore, a smart lessor would either keep the ITC and reduce the lessee monthly payment to be competitive with bank loans or increase their yield.

Another significant event occurred in 1963, when the Comptroller of the Currency issued a ruling permitting banks to get into the leasing business. Before this, national banks were not allowed to own or lease personal property since their business was restricted to lending money. Previous involvement in leasing had been limited mainly to the trustee function involving equipment trust certificates. As soon as banks began to take an active role in equipment leasing, the use of equipment trust certificates began to fade.

The escalating war in Vietnam during the late 1960s affected both the social and economic fiber of American life. The Treasury steadily increased its borrowings to finance defense spending and social programs, pushing interest rates on both federal and corporate debt instruments up to the 7 percent and 8 percent levels.

By 1968 the federal deficit had reached $25 billion.

Congress began using ITC to prod the economy in whichever direction seemed appropriate, with the following results:

> *1962 - ITC introduced*
> *1966 - repealed*
> *1967 - re-enacted*
> *1969 - repealed*
> *1971 - re-enacted*
> *1986 - repealed*

This flip-flop of tax benefits along with rising interest rates gave the leasing industry its first taste of its love/hate relationship with the government.

The year 1970 ushered in a turbulent decade for the economy. The continued emphasis on defense spending and the push for technological advancement left the government with an increasing budget deficit, declining GNP and growing unemployment.

In August of 1971, President Nixon imposed the first peacetime wage and price controls. This resulted in companies jacking up their prices and then discounting them for selected customers in order to stay within the confines of the law. By 1973 the Watergate scandal and the Arab oil embargo had twice caused devaluation of the U.S. dollar.

The prime rate steadily increased during this decade, from 6 percent to 15.75 percent. Inflation rose to 12 percent, discouraging savings and reducing capital available for investment. Corporate profits were sharply reduced, and the economy slid deeper into recession. Research and development, investment in new equipment and the planned replacement of aging assets were usually the first budget items to be cut.

Congress responded by reinstating ITC in 1971, then increasing the ITC rate from 7 percent to 10 percent in 1975. In 1972, Congress introduced Asset Depreciation Ranges (ADR). This law created hundreds of asset categories and prescribed useful lives for depreciating assets. Before this, lessors had to guess the useful life of the asset, and if a lessor chose a shorter life than the IRS thought reasonable, the lessor would lose the depreciation benefits.

Banks were given a stronger foothold in the leasing industry when Congress amended the Bank Holding Company Act in 1970. This amendment allowed banks to form holding companies and bank subsidiaries. As subsidiaries, bank leasing companies were no longer subject to the stringent reserve requirements of their parent banks, providing them with more financial leverage and greater profits.

Companies like IBM and Xerox began to use leasing more widely to finance the distribution of their products. They maintained equipment title, offered shorter terms, and re-marketed the equipment after the lease. These benefits attracted many customers who wanted to avoid the risk of computer and copier technical obsolescence. Vendor leasing quickly spread to other types of equipment, including office machinery and furniture, cash registers, and restaurant equipment.

The marketplace also created new types of products. One example is the leveraged lease, a highly sophisticated product that combines three parties — lessor, lessee and lender. In this type of transaction, the lessor finances the equipment by putting in 20 percent equity and borrowing 80 percent from a lender on a non-recourse basis. The lessor then keeps all of the tax benefits as well as deducts the interest on the loan. The leveraged tax benefits allow the lessor to offer the lessee extremely low rentals while maintaining a high yield.

Since the complex structuring of leveraged leases was not foreseen in 1955, many lessors required private tax rulings from the IRS. In 1975, the IRS responded by issuing Revenue Procedure 75-21. This procedure amplified its 1955 ruling and specified in more detail what criteria would be used to govern leasing transactions for tax purposes.

Under Revenue Procedure 75-21, five conditions had to be met to assure a favorable ruling:

1. The lessor must maintain a minimal "at risk" investment of 20 percent during the term of the lease

2. The term of the lease must include all renewal or extension periods, except for optional renewal periods, at prevailing fair market value
3. Lessee may not purchase the asset at less than fair market value
4. The lessee may not furnish any part of the cost of the asset
5. The lessor must expect a profit from the transaction apart from the tax benefits of ownership

While the IRS was dealing with the tax aspects of lessors, the Securities and Exchange Commission (SEC) was concerned with inconsistent lessor balance sheets and income statements. They wanted to standardize the financial statement reporting methods of both lessors and lessees in order to help investors make better-informed investment decisions. In 1976, the Financial Accounting Standards Board (FASB), under pressure by the SEC, issued a comprehensive lease accounting document entitled Financial Accounting Statement No. 13 (FASB 13).

This statement classifies a lease as either a capital lease or an operating lease from the lessee's viewpoint. If the lease is determined to be a capital lease, the lessee must account for it as an outright purchase and show the asset in their financial statements. An operating lease, on the other hand, is not reflected on the balance sheet and future rentals are disclosed only in the footnotes.

Lessors are subjected to similar tests designed to create accounting symmetry, but these criteria leave some loopholes that make it possible for both parties to leave the asset off the balance sheet.

In the 80s, the leasing industry witnessed five major tax laws in a very short period of time:

- Economic Recovery and Tax Act of 1981 (ERTA)
- Tax Equity and Fiscal Responsibility Act of 1982 (TEFRA)
- Deficit Reduction Act of 1984 (DRA)
- Tax Reform Act of 1986 (TRA)
- Competitive Bank Equality Act of 1987 (CEBA)

In August of 1981, Congress passed ERTA, an extensive revision of the 1954 Internal Revenue Code. Led by a Republican majority in the Senate, Congress believed that the private sector would spend and invest more money and stimulate the economy if tax burdens could be sharply reduced.

Two features of this law had major impacts on leasing (1) ACRS - Accelerated Cost Recovery System and (2) Safe Harbor Leasing.

ACRS replaced the complex ADR depreciation system with a simpler and faster cost recovery system. This new system contained only five classes of assets ranging from 3-year to 15-year life spans and specified the percentage of cost to be written off in each year. This enabled an owner/lessor to fully depreciate an asset without having to estimate useful life and salvage value.

Safe harbor leasing had a major impact on the entire business community. Tax benefits were made available to lessors other than those complying with "true lease" guidelines. Only three tests had to be met to qualify for the tax benefits of ownership:

1. Lessor is a corporation (excluding subchapter S and personal holding companies)
2. Lessor's minimum investment in the leased asset is never less than 10 percent (reduced from 20 percent)
3. The term of the lease does not exceed 90 percent of the useful life of the asset or 150 percent of the class life of the asset.

If all of these requirements were satisfied, the transaction would qualify as a lease for tax purposes regardless of other factors previously disallowed, like bargain purchase options and limited-use property.

Another new feature of safe harbor leasing was the tax benefit transfer (TBT) lease. This enabled lessors to structure a lease with direct matching of incoming rentals and debt payments to make a single payment to the lessee for the tax benefits. This aspect of the law led quickly to major sales of tax shelters to "nominal lessors" who were not normally in the leasing business. Several major companies like General Electric, IBM and AT&T, did not pay taxes that year due to their tremendous participation in the TBT marketplace.

As soon as it was enacted in 1981, ERTA became a scapegoat for the continually *rising federal budget deficit. The volume of leases written jumped from $32.8 billion in 1979 to $57.6 billion in 1982, creating an unforeseen loss of tax revenues.*

Congress passed TEFRA in August of 1982 to increase tax revenues lost under ERTA. This new act repealed safe harbor leasing and replaced it with the "finance lease", along with a complicated phase-in schedule. It also introduced the "90-day window", allowing leases to be written on new equipment already in service.

The finance lease liberalized the "true lease" guidelines of Revenue Procedure 75-21 in one major respect - fixed price purchase options of at least 10 percent would qualify for lease consideration. It also contained some unfavorable requirements - spreading the ITC benefits over 5 years and limiting the amount of tax liability that could be offset by ITC.

Although interest and inflation rates had returned to acceptable ranges by 1984, the budget deficit was growing enormously and had become a political hot potato. In June of 1984, Congress passed the Deficit Reduction Act in at attempt to raise tax revenue.

This new act postponed the introduction of finance leases from January 1984 until January 1988, as Congress recognized the impact on the Treasury of the rapidly growing leasing industry.

The Deficit Reduction Act of 1984 affected the leasing industry in several other ways:

- *Time value of money was introduced by requiring lessors to adjust uneven rental streams for tax purposes*
- *Depreciation benefits on real property were reduced*
- *True-tax treatment was disallowed for leases to foreign corporations not subject to U.S. income tax*
- *TRAC leases, primarily affecting the vehicle leasing industry, were recognized as true-tax leases*

In December 1984, President Reagan submitted a proposal to Congress for tax simplification. Some of the aspects of this proposal, especially the elimination of the investment tax credit, caused some concern within the leasing industry. That concern finally came to pass with the signing of the Tax Reform Act in October of 1986.

This tax change was so complicated that it required 2000 pages to document it. Major changes affecting leasing included:

- *Repealing the Investment Tax Credit*
- *Lengthening equipment useful lives*
- *Introducing an alternative minimum tax*
- *Reducing depreciable amounts in the earlier years.*

In 1987, Congress decided to help the banking community compete more effectively against the independent leasing companies in the operating lease market by passing the Competitive Bank Equality Act of 1987. In this legislation, Congress allowed major financial institutions to put up to 10 percent of their assets into operating leases. Prior to this new law, banks could not provide this type of lease due to the perceived risks and costs of direct ownership.

Nonetheless, few banks took advantage of this opportunity and many left the equipment leasing industry altogether. In fact, independent leasing firms began to move into other aspects of structured asset finance to take advantage of banks' reluctance to avoid high-risk projects.

At the same time, FASB enacted four major rulings that dramatically changed how leasing companies operated.

1. **FASB 91:** *required leasing companies to reduce the amount of initial direct costs eligible to be booked at lease inception.*
2. **FASB 94**: *required leasing companies to consolidate their leasing subsidiaries activities with the parent company.*
3. **FASB 95:** *required leasing companies to produce cash flow statements instead of source and use of funds statements and*
4. **FASB 96**: *overhauled income tax/deferred tax computations and presentation.*

From 1988 to 1995 the equipment industry went through some extremely difficult times. The industry leading newspapers ran monthly headlines such as, "Survival *in the 90's", and "The Lessor Under Chapter 11". Article 2A of the Uniform Commercial Code, which codified leasing transactions, was initially adopted in 17 states. And the Equipment Leasing Association (ELA) was losing members left and right.*

Finally, in the mid 90s Wall Street and the business community discovered the Internet and the IPO market. It was almost impossible not to make money. Companies were expanding quickly. High-tech communities in California, Texas and Massachusetts supplied talent to automate every process possible. The word E-lease was invented and volume went through the roof. Under President Clinton the economy grew more than 4-5 percent per year. Companies such as Sun, HP, IBM, and Cisco became household names and started their own captive finance companies.

Unfortunately, the party could not last forever. Alan Greenspan lowered the federal borrowing rate 9 times to an all-time low of 2.5 percent to offset a growing recession.

As a result of Sept. 11 and the limping economy, Congress passed The Job Creation and Worker Assistance Act of 2002, which created a new concept called "bonus depreciation". Retroactive to Sept 11 of 2001, bonus depreciation provides an additional 30 percent first-year tax depreciation (before declaring regular MACRS) to a tax owner of qualified new equipment. The basis of the property and subsequent depreciation benefits are reduced to reflect this "bonus".

Prior to the enactment of this new tax provision, many lessors thought that bonus depreciation would help leasing. Unfortunately, feedback from the lessor community indicates that this may or may not be true, depending on the tax life of the asset.

In general, small-ticket and middle-market players reported little or no impact from the bonus depreciation whereas large ticket players reported some positive impact in their pricing. Yet, many large ticket players said that they were hurt by an inability to syndicate the tax benefits.

Many lessors feel that the economy has slowed the need for equipment financing and that surplus equipment and rental companies are competing heavily against new purchases. Accounting scandals have scarred off-balance sheet financing, and

CFOs are demanding on-balance sheets with no footnote disclosures. In addition, low interest rates from banks and manufacturer incentive programs favor financing.

Our industry is in trouble. We may be down, but we are not out. We are just going through another phase of leasing evolution. Good times are always followed by bad times, which are followed by good times. The question is, how long do the bad times last? History indicates 7-10 years.

I've always looked to GE for guidance because I believed that if GE was doing well then things had to be good. They have, traditionally, had the most expensive pricing in our industry and lessees were willing to pay for the product, service and name.

Then Enron came along and changed the world. Common things like Special Purpose Entities (SPEs), commercial paper conduits (CP) and aggressive accounting went out of favor with the investment community.

Arthur Andersen lost more than 500 clients ($1 billion billings) since the Enron meltdown and eventually went out of business.

Forty six of the 50 states lost precious tax revenue and are approaching poverty status.

Real estate lessors reported that fewer leases are being renewed or are renewed at substantially lower rates.

Patents on blockbuster drugs, including Procardia and Zocor have expired. Managed-care companies are successfully pushing patients away from high-priced new drugs toward cheap generics. In the long term, the newest treatments promise to get more expensive, as the industry invests more in research and development and gets less out of it. The likely outcome is worsening battles among the drug industry, managed-care companies, and federal and state governments over drug prices.

IBM, which has one of the largest captive finance companies in the world, laid off 10,000 people or 2.5 percent of their worldwide force.

And, the International Accounting Standards Board (IASB) published proposals to revise 12 of its 34 active standards, thus forcing the issue of accounting harmonization across the globe.

The world is getting smaller and it's getting more crowded. Everyone wants to get their two cents in. And there are going to be some big time losers in the next couple of years. It does not matter whether you live in the US or China.

Welcome to the Leasing Industry!
Next Chapter: Where are the Leaders?

Chapter 3

WHERE ARE THE LEADERS?

Over the years, some of the best talent in the world has avoided our industry and instead chosen investment banking, banking, arbitrage or dot-coms. As a result, those of us who chose this field had to work with string, bubble gum, a wing and a prayer to win over confidence with our clients.

When leasing was a third-rate product back in the 50s, this industry attracted a lot of "sleazy" personalities who wanted a piece of the 36 percent – 48 percent yield action. Presidents of companies did not need to learn leadership.

All they had to do was hire young, aggressive, commission-oriented people, give them the "yellow" pages and say "start calling".

It was a game of numbers. Make the perquisite number of phone calls and you would win the business. Rarely did the accountants, tax professionals or lawyers get involved. In a way, life was simple.

As our society becomes more competitive and Internet-connected and the older generation of leasing leadership retires, new and tough demands are put on the leasing leaders of tomorrow. Additionally, mergers and acquisitions roar over the landscape, creating vacuums in leadership.

Leasing leaders today have so many challenges that it is nearly impossible to deal effectively with all of them. They have to survive with a world economy that misbehaves. They must face FASB and the IASB, which keep trying to shut down off-balance-sheet financing, SPEs and off-shore vehicles. And if that were not enough, they must endure a U.S. Congress and the SEC who have consistently and clearly demonstrated anti-corporate tendencies to show the world that we will get rid of every rule and regulation that allowed the occurrence of such disasters as Enron, Tyco, Global Crossing, WorldCom and Imclone.

Many of us who went to business school were trained to be managers, not leaders. Leaders must cope with change and that requires unconventional originality which is counterintuitive. Leaders also have to deal with complex issues that force them to live by a set of ethical rules that have never been formally designated by any authority.

I remember sitting for my CPA exam back in the 70s — failed twice and passed the third time. Even after all that hard work, I still failed the ethics exam. Every time I saw a way to make money, I said I would do it. And, of course, I would learn that it was unethical. To pass the exam, I had to think differently, not naturally.

Many leading business psychologists agree that tomorrow's successful leaders need to possess the following characteristics:

- International background and work experience
- Strong family influence
- Honest and trustworthy
- Flexible and adaptable

If you do not have the above characteristics, that does not mean that you cannot rise as a leader. It just means that it may be harder.

Leaders must foster, recognize and reward excellent work. Lessors need to rethink current sales compensation schemes and reformulate them for "ethics nouveau." Here are some ideas that you may want to incorporate into your own leasing company:

- Targets met
- Sales accomplished
- Savings gained
- Customer compliments received
- First account opened in each industry
- First repeat order from every new account
- Under-budget completion of important projects

- *Innovations that save money*
- *Fastest cycle time to date*
- *Shortest time to respond*
- *Most productive shift*
- *Most consistent performance*

Eleven Unhealthy Leadership Behavior Patterns

Finally, too many of our current leasing leaders demonstrate behavior patterns that I believe disrupt healthy conversations among the sales force. If you demonstrate several of these powerful emotions on a consistent basis, you may need to change your patterns or you, too, may find yourself facing a trial by jury or a coup.

1. VOLATILE

People who are volatile tend to be moody and unpredictable. They erupt suddenly with outbursts of strong emotion, usually with little warning. Volatile leaders may be enthusiastic one moment, doubtful and despairing the next. They are hard to predict or anticipate. It is difficult to trust or rely on them because of sudden shifts between excessive enthusiasm and strong reservations.

2. DISTRUSTFUL

They offend easily and are highly skeptical of others' motives. They look for hidden agendas and disguised signals. They are suspicious and dubious about others. They downplay future possibilities or assume that things will not turn out well, often resisting change with a tendency to over-criticize.

3. OVERLY CAUTIOUS

Overly cautious leaders are unassertive, with a tendency to brood excessively, worry and second-guess decisions. They fear making mistakes, creating indecisiveness or inaction. Often, they will ask for an overabundance of information and overly study issues before taking action. They preoccupy their thoughts with "what could go wrong" and spend excessive time contemplating negative "what ifs".

4. ALOOF

They do not care about the feelings of others. They do not get involved emotionally. Seen as withdrawn and aloof, they lack empathy or concern. They avoid conflict, withdraw, and do not provide communication or feedback. They may "show up" but not actually "be there."

5. PASSIVE RESISTANT

They seem to cooperate and agree but, privately, they maintain reservations and concerns. In meetings, they appear to go along with decisions but then, independently, pursue their own agenda. In public they agree, but privately they are irritable, resentful, stubborn and resistant, finding ways to circumvent agreements or commitments, usually for "good reasons."

6. ARROGANT

Arrogant leaders powerfully show their self-confidence with feelings of entitlement and inflated views of self-worth and ability. Convinced of the correctness of their opinion, they will belittle or diminish the input of others and show disdain for other views.

7. MISCHIEVIOUS

A mischievous leader has the skill to test limits, seek excitement and take risks. They will push the boundaries of possibilities and sometimes "walk the line" of acceptable or ethical conduct. They are very willing to act in underhanded ways in order to accomplish their vision or mission.

8. MELODRAMATIC

They expect to be liked and enjoy being the center of attention. They like to perform and command through extreme bravado, confidence, and sometimes domination, often acting out with the intent of self-attention. They will even create crises, to show off their leadership skills.

9. ECCENTRIC

Eccentric leaders act, think, and communicate in odd and unusual ways. These leaders go out of their way to get reactions from others. They like to shake things up when nothing is required, bewildering staff along the way.

10. PERFECTIONISTIC

Precise, meticulous and compulsively conscientious, they are concerned about details, form, and the complete elimination of mistakes, mishaps, or chaos. They will micro-manage entire teams of employees and fail to delegate even the smallest level of detail.

11. PLEASER

They are eager to meet the expectations of others, reluctant to take independent action or go against the opinion of others. They want to satisfy others and avoid conflict or disappointment. They will not stick up for their direct reports and staff, thus setting up people for the kill.

It is my experience that most leaders exhibit multi-faceted combinations of these traits and change from time to time to adapt to the issues of the days. It is not humanly possible to stay the course constantly. We are not machines.

Welcome to the Leasing Industry!
Next Chapter: Are You Ready to Learn?

Chapter 4

ARE YOU READY TO LEARN?

According to historians, ancient Greeks regarded feelings as being too individual or self-centered to be reliable; thus, wise people admitted no emotion. On the other hand, in 18th century Europe, romantics believed feelings could produce insights that logic couldn't.

It has been my experience that in the modern corporation, emotions are usually stifled and viewed as disruptive. Violators are accused of "wearing emotions on their sleeves." As a result of this cultural herding, leasing companies lose some of their best talent to more creative environments.

Emotions enhance business decisions, promote creative thinking and yield better-than-average profits. By ignoring emotions, lessors set themselves up to fall apart in the long-term.

Psychology professors John Mayer and Peter Salovey pioneered the study of Emotional Intelligence (EI) with an academic paper in 1990 that defined EI as: "the ability to perceive emotions, to access and generate emotions so as to assist thought, to understand emotions and emotional knowledge, and to reflectively regulate emotions so as to promote emotional and intellectual thought".

Emotional Intelligence makes us smarter by integrating our head with our heart. In their breakthrough paper, they identify four major concepts that leasing professionals can use to optimize sales:

- *Identify emotions accurately – i.e. recognizing inconsistencies in people's body language*
- *Facilitate emotions – i.e. using emotions to motivate others*

- *Understand emotions — i.e. processing mixed messages and diffusing potential conflicts*
- *Manage emotions — i.e. controlling feelings in order to devise effective strategies*

They conclude that the regulation of emotions does not require the suppression of feelings. They hypothesize that moderating negative emotions while enhancing positive ones leads to more success, fosters positive corporate cultures and maximizes entrepreneurial possibilities.

Emotional Intelligence is particularly important in the first stages of entrepreneurial activities. Even though something may look impossible, people with high EI have an instinct that drives them forward. Non-believers think that high EI people are crazy.

If you believe in EI, you gauge people by how they dress, how they sound, and how they handle themselves. You look at personal qualities like initiative, empathy, adaptability and persuasiveness.

Major research indicates that only a small part of success at work is due to technical ability (20 percent) and that most success can be attributed to workers' EI (80 percent).

If you follow EI and your company does not, watch out. Engaging lessees and vendors at an emotional level can only take place if everything within the leasing organization is set up to give them a positive experience.

In other words, one "Oh _____" can do a lot of damage to hundreds of "Yeahs".

Motivation to learn

We're living in incredibly turbulent times. The rapid rate of change buffets both lessors and lessees, making it extremely difficult to achieve success. It's no wonder that we're confused and uncertain about what to do. And John Nesbitt, the futurist, has predicted that in the year 2020, the rate of knowledge will double every 35 days! That means it is likely that the conclusions, paradigms and core beliefs upon which we based our decisions just two or three years ago are likely to be obsolete today. Even more sobering, the conclusions and strategies which we develop today will be obsolete in a couple of years.

An insightful person will accept that rapid change is now a defining characteristic of our economy, and deal with it effectively on an on-going basis as a way of life.

What's the best way to go forward in the light of this rapid change? What mindsets and skills can we adopt that will equip us to survive and prosper in turbulent times and the hyper-information age?

Self-Directed Learning Key to Success

I believe there is one core skill which will define the most successful individuals. It's the ability and propensity to engage in self-directed learning. The only sustainable effective response to a rapidly changing world is cultivating the ability to positively transform ourselves and our organizations. And that's the definition of self-directed learning.

The individuals who become disciplined, systematic self-directed learners will be the success stories of this new era. Likewise, those organizations that become learning organizations have the best chance of surviving and prospering.

In a nutshell, the only competitive advantage the leasing company of the future will have is its manager's ability to learn faster than their competitor. In fact, I would argue that the rate at which individuals and organizations learn may become the only sustainable competitive advantage.

In a world that is rapidly changing (i.e. government intervention), today's hot new product is tomorrow's obsolete dinosaur (i.e. synthetic leases).

As the economy becomes more and more global, competition increases. Few businesses will enjoy a secure market position. The quality of competition will also improve as competitors strive to outperform one another in providing customer service with value-added products and services. In this new economy, those who survive and prosper will be those who know how to learn faster and more systematically than their competitors.

Seven Learning Inhibitors:

I have learned that we do certain things, periodically, that minimize the effectiveness of our learning experiences. Try to avoid the following:

- *Snap judgments*

  Often we react quickly to information without thinking through the problem. It is OK to wait and make a decision after you have gathered more information. As difficult as it may be, it is not OK to postpone making a decision forever.

- *Reliance on a select "few"*

  Senior executives tend to make this mistake. They tend to rely on the "few" people that they have entrusted for years. If they venture outside the box, they either feel uncomfortable or do not want to alienate their closest "friends".

- *Prejudiced observations*

  No matter how intelligent you are, you bring a certain amount of prejudice to the table every time you make a decision. We can undo a lot of "baggage" and dysfunctional viewpoints that we inherited, but we can not undo all of the years of negative experience that we acquired through our friends, relatives, bosses, clients, vendors, and the like.

- *Fault-finding*

  It so much easier to blame someone else, rather than criticize oneself. That is why so many people do it.

- *Overlooking achievements*

  To be successful, you need to rely on others to help you. If you overlook their achievements, as small as they may seem to you, you will lose your support team and your connections to success.

- *Promoting negativity*

  Every so often, I am asked for an opinion and I give it freely. Sometimes, my readers do not like my honesty and frankness. They sometimes say that I am harsh and should not air dirty laundry in public. Although I may disagree with them, it is wrong, inappropriate and unprofessional to promote negativity to anyone. It is better to say nothing.

- *Failure to return phone calls or e-mails*

  I believe that everyone should respond to all phone calls and e-mails. I do not understand why people start a relationship and then, all of a sudden, stop communicating. I've never understood why people think that they cannot find the time to make the call. How long does it take to pick up the telephone, dial a number, wait for three rings and leave a message? Thirty seconds, max. And, all you have to say is "I want to stop communicating with you."

Achievement Blockers

I have met many leasing professionals, who have the uncanny ability to succeed — but don't. They make their numbers most of the time and are admired by their peers and management. Although they deal with day-to-day problems fairly well, they sometimes miss out on opportunities which could accelerate their careers or put more money in their pockets.

In most cases they do not know what they are doing to hurt their career or do not know how they come across to others. It is because no one ever told them.

Here are the tell-tale signs of professionals who block their own achievements:

- **Lack purpose and passion**

  If you are going to work 70 hours a week you'd better love what you are doing. Each day you awake, you should feel purpose and passion. When you stop feeling either of the two, it's time to either look at alternative jobs or try a new life style.

- **Show no ability to adapt**

  This person is already successful and does not want to change for fear that she will lose something that she has already earned.

- **Cannot change in response to crisis**

  This person watches the ship go down and hopes that someone will save him before going under for the third time.

- **Tolerate unsatisfactory situations and relationships**

  I've often argued that one has to let go of the past in order to make room for the new. This person stays in bad situations which prevent him from moving forward.

- **Stop at the edge of uncharted waters**

  Number one people do not have a map for success. They invent as they go along. When they come to uncharted waters they are forced to make decisions. They must either go into the water, build a bridge to cross it, go around it, or head back to their last resting point.

- **Ignore important relationships**

  On the road to success, many people will ignore clients and family. You cannot ignore either. You must sell yourselves to your existing clients and take care of your family because, at the end of the day, they will be the only ones around to share your moments of trouble.

- ***Forget to have fun***

  You cannot leave your inner child behind, because it is with you for now and forever. If you cannot remember the last time you laughed, stop reading this book right now and go do something that will make you laugh.

- ***Look to others for job satisfaction and feedback***

  Forget about the "boss" or "friend" who will satisfy your needs. There were times, many many years ago, when you could call a boss or friend and spend quality time. Nowadays, everyone is busy and compliments have disappeared. Successful people need to find satisfaction within themselves. And this is not easy for a salesperson, who loves to be on stage.

- ***Listen too much to one's "inner critic"***

  I have met a lot of people who say that they did something stupid. Or they will criticize themselves while re-enacting a particular situation that did not go as well as expected. I find that this exercise wastes too much energy and does not accomplish anything.

In summary, your learning goals should incorporate the following challenges:

- *Increase your emotional intelligence*
- *Live with and enjoy a world of constant change*
- *Avoid activities which disrupt learning*
- *Destroy all achievement blockers*

It is not enough to just want to learn. One has to prioritize it and incorporate it into daily life. You need to rearrange your current responsibilities to make room for new knowledge. If you don't clean out your brain closet to make room, you'll never retain what you've learned.

Chapter 5

WHY COMPANIES LEASE?

Leasing is an expensive product. It is more expensive than cash or loans. Therefore, it is very important to understand why a lessee would want to choose a more expensive product.

No one favors Mercedes or Tiffany for low prices. Similarly, lessees are not looking for a bargain when they choose leasing. They choose it for its unique benefits and advantages.

Leasing benefits can be summarized as follows:

- **Accounting**

  Lease accounting is governed by FASB 13 in the US. Adopted in July, 1976 FASB 13 has been the primary method for allowing lessees to keep operating leases off their balance sheets. By keeping the rentals off the balance sheet the lessee achieves a better Return on Asset (ROA) which is net income after tax/assets (NIAT). Leveraging ratios, such as debt/equity, also improve because the liability is not on the balance sheet.

  Since operating leases are rentals, they are usually paid for out of the operating budgets, thus minimizing utilization of capital budgets.

  Another advantage is that many divisions in the field avoid or reduce headquarter overhead charges because the allocation formula looks at assets, which are now off balance sheet.

  Unfortunately, since Enron, off-balance-sheet financing has been under attack.

And, many CFOs are requiring on balance sheet treatment. Enron's abuse of off-balance sheet treatment scarred leasing and no one knows, at this point, whether it is temporary or permanent.

Many CFOs today would rather have the asset and the liability on the balance sheet, take the ROA hit and avoid investors thinking that they are hiding something. Say the word footnote, and they will show you to the door.

- **Tax**

Rentals are tax deductible under Section 162 of the US tax code. Unlike a loan, where the interest is only tax-deductible, a lessee can deduct the entire amount as a rental. Often, a lessee will opt for a shorter term thus compressing the tax advantages.

If the lessee has tax ownership (i.e. finance lease), they will take bonus depreciation, MACRS and interest expense. If they are eligible, they will claim a Sec. 179 deduction.

Some lessees are very aggressive and request a step-down lease, which again accelerates the tax deductions into the earlier years. Section 467 of the tax code contains a rule called 90/110, which says that the lowest rent cannot be less than 90 percent of the average rent and the highest rent cannot be more than 110 percent of the average rent. Currently, transactions which have aggregate rent of $2,000,000 or less are exempt from this test. If you violate the 90/110 test and don't qualify for the exemption, you may owe taxes to the IRS.

- **Financial reasons**

Traditionally, leasing companies have taken on tougher credits than the banks. Unfortunately, banks have tightened their lending standards to leasing companies and lessors have had to pull back as lender of last resort.

Still, leasing companies do provide more credit since we base our decisions not only on the value of the asset/collateral but on how the lessee plans to use the equipment to grow their business and generate more income to pay for the lease.

Lessors serve as an additional source of capital, thus allowing the lessee to not tie up their working capital in equipment.

- **Cash management**

Lessors strive to structure transactions that minimize monthly cash flow by taking residual risk. By doing so, lessees can acquire more equipment for less money. By lowering the payment, lessees free up cash to use elsewhere in their business. This is commonly called "maximizing a lessee's liquidity preference."

In addition, lessors will finance down payments, installation of new equipment, de-installation of used equipment, warranties, sales tax, consultants and other expenditures necessary to carry out the project.

- **Technological obsolescence**

One of the key reasons lessees lease is due to their perception of technological obsolescence. By leasing the equipment, instead of owning it, a lessee can create a predictable and cost-effective path for upgrades, refinancings, and tech refreshes.

To support this desire, lessors have created or outsourced cost efficient "refurb" factories that take back used equipment, refurbish it and put it back on the market as quickly as possible.

- **Ownership**

Ownership may have its privileges but it also has its costs. In the US, most equipment is taxed once a year under the property tax laws. In several states, there are additional excise taxes. Since leasing is a rental concept, often these taxes can either be avoided or financed by the lessor.

Partnerships and joint ventures prefer rentals since they can dispose of the assets at the time of break-up by simply sending the equipment back to the lessor.

In addition, most lessees do not want to delve into the world of disposal and salvage. Many see it as a hassle and do not have the expertise or core competency to maximize resale value.

- ### *Service and flexibility*

Lessors try to close financing at the time of equipment purchase, either through captive finance programs or vendor private label programs. This, in essence, assures one-stop shopping and convenience.

Experience indicates that lessors can finance many auxiliary services, such as sales tax, property tax, maintenance, insurance and extended warranties, as bundled services resulting in lower administrative costs to the lessee.

Through lease structuring, lessors can tailor transactions to meet the unique cash flow requirements of the lessee. Although level rents are the most common, step-up and deferred rent structures satisfy start-up companies, step-down leases increase tax deductions and skip leases target businesses with seasonal cash flows.

Vendor motivation is slightly different. They are more motivated by the following:

- ### *Market Control*

Vendors love to control their markets by maximizing prices and minimizing inventory. Leasing helps create the initial sale by eliminating the focus on the purchase price or list-price discounting. Financing allows more sales to be closed since it makes it easier for the lessee to acquire the use of the equipment without having to pay for it.

During the term, vendors utilize the monthly invoice to send messages to lessees telling them about special offerings such as upgrades and tech refreshes.

Again, at the end of the term, a vendor has tighter control about disposition options, since the lessee or the vendor may want to buy the equipment from the lessor. This option controls the prices in the secondary market.

- **Market Enhancement**

Vendors can make more money through active leasing programs. Often, they will want to participate in the financing or in taking residual risk. Full service leasing allows a vendor to provide pre-paid maintenance contracts and specialty programs such as fuel monitoring.

In some cases, lessors will provide additional funds to take out the existing lease transaction.

Vendors will typically want to enter into full-service remarketing programs, since lessors do not want to house equipment between transactions. Vendors will also enter into repurchase agreements, whereby they agree to buy back the lessee's contracts.

Never sell leasing on price, ROA or APR. To maximize your commissions, sell the lease on its inherent benefits and advantages.

Chapter 6

THE LIFECYCLE OF A LEASE

Like people, equipment leases have a life of their own.

- **PRE-BOOKING** – *prepping the lessee*
- **FUNDING** - *the lease is born*
- **SERVICING** – *as long as the lessee uses the equipment, you will have a relationship with them*
- **TERMINATION** - *sometimes leases end their lives naturally; most of the time they don't.*

If you are going to be successful in sales, you will need to have a thorough understanding of the following activities:

- *Find customers – we discuss this in more detail later in the book*
- *Book transactions - account for leases*
- *Dispose of the equipment – re-lease it or sell it outright through various marketing channels.*

PRE-BOOKING

Before a lease is booked, a great deal of organizational effort must happen in four distinct areas within the equipment leasing organization:

- *Marketing & Sales*
- *Application Processing*
- *Credit Investigation*
- *Documentation*

Marketing & Sales

You and your sales support group are responsible for finding potential lessees. You will work with management to achieve the optimal product mix, market orientation and marketing strategy.

To determine the proper leasing mix, management looks at its own tax appetite, local competition, the quality/experience of the existing sales force, and the content of the existing portfolio. It then outlines a detailed business plan and will instruct you to develop a marketing plan.

Your marketing department will determine the most profitable market by analyzing conditions such as the local economy, competition, and pricing structures. This is often done with on-site, telephone and formal consulting surveys. After reviewing this information, the marketing department produces a plan of attack consistent with management's business objectives (MBO).

You then must lay out a detailed agenda for securing customers. Possible approaches include trade shows, advertising, direct mail, telephone surveys, bank correspondent relationships, service bureau affiliations, equipment vendors, accounts, lawyers, insurance professionals and the Chamber of Commerce.

Application Processing

Your primary job is completed when the potential lessee has completed an application for a lease. The application usually contains information about the lessee, the equipment being considered, how the lessee will use it, and the terms of the proposed lease.

The lease application should be dated. Today most of the Internet-based solutions automate this process in the field. Many leasing companies keep track of the time it takes for an application to become a lease. This is called turnaround time. In an especially competitive marketplace, the lessor with the fastest document turnaround time usually gets the business.

As applications go through this step, they are checked for valid customer identification numbers, SIC/NAIC industry codes and equipment classification codes. These codes are important to management, since they indicate the type of business that is attracted to the company.

Credit Investigation

Credit investigation, leading to approval or rejection, represents the critical point in the lease's life cycle. Although automated credit models are being installed at an ever-quickening pace, it takes highly qualified credit analysts to judge the creditworthiness of lessees. Because leases require multiple payments over long periods of time, a lessee's financial condition and payment habits must be closely scrutinized.

Some lessors have developed credit scoring systems to standardize this review process. This objective approach can improve efficiency in evaluating most credit, but it should be used with caution. Mitigating circumstances that arise in each customer's situation might not be judged properly by a scoring system. In these cases, the credit analyst should be allowed to override the scoring system and justify his/her decision.

When an application reaches a credit analyst, she will thoroughly analyze the credit information and research the customer's background through the use of credit bureaus like D&B, Fairlsaacs, TRW and Experian. Typically, a potentially bad customer will already have a history of slow or bad payments, frequent relocation and name changes.

When the credit analyst has completed her review of the application, she will mark the application with one of the following decisions:

- **Approval** - the lease is approved subject to the completion of the required documentation
- **Conditional Approval** - some leases are approved subject to additional guarantees, covenants and other forms of security
- **Decline** - if the lessee is judged to be a risk greater than the lessor's tolerance

level, the application is rejected

- **Return for more information** - *sometimes important information is left off the application, or the standard information is not enough for a credit decision. This often occurs in borderline credit situations. The application usually goes back to you so that you can contact the potential lessee for the missing information.*

In some of the larger organizations, a pending credit will be sent to someone with higher credit authority. Many times, the size of the deal determines which approval level is necessary.

Documentation

Leases require a tremendous amount of paperwork to document agreements, stipulations, promises, and events like equipment delivery. For the leasing company's protection, it must closely monitor the documentation process to make sure all these documents are in order. Each lease may have different requirements, depending on the type of lease, type or cost of equipment, lessee credit rating, and vendor program agreements.

The documentation department should first determine that the lessee has fulfilled his requirements, which often includes the receipt of a lessee advance payment. At this point, the leasing company issues a purchase order and notifies the vendor to deliver the equipment to the lessee.

After the equipment is inspected by the lessee, she signs a delivery & acceptance (D&A) certificate stating that the equipment is in good working order. The leasing company may then pay the vendor. However, verbal confirmation with the lessee to assure her satisfaction with the equipment is often a good additional step for the lessor to take before paying the vendor.

FUNDING

The lease is ready to fund. Funding is a rather time-consuming process, but it's better to take a few precautionary steps to determine the integrity of the lease rather than rush to get it on the books.

Let's summarize what has to happen to an application before it is ready to fund:

- *Application completed*
- *Lessee credit approved*
- *All necessary lessee documents received*
- *Advance rental received*
- *Lease signed*
- *Equipment delivery verified with lessee*

During the funding stage, a lot of information is captured for the following areas:

- *Lease accounting*
- *Lessee billing*
- *Lease tracking*
- *Equipment tracking*

These categories represent different service functions in a leasing organization. Most of this information should be available from the documentation gathered in the lease file.

Most leasing organizations have a monthly business cycle. This means that approved leases must be captured as quickly a possible in order to post to the proper accounting period.

In most sales organizations where performance and compensation are tied directly to sales volume, there is a huge push at the end of the month to meet sales goals.

There are some other critical tasks performed during the funding stage:

- ***UCC filings*** *- most lessors file UCCs (within 10 days) with the state or county where the equipment is located.*
- ***Insurance requirements*** *- the lessor should protect himself against damage or loss of the leased equipment as well as liability associated with its use. Since the lessee has possession of the equipment, the lease should require*

the lessee to include the lessor in his insurance policy.

Finally, we book our lease.

SERVICING

Unlike products in most industries, a lease transaction does not end with the sale. When we fund a lease, we live with it for a long time.

1. Billing and Collections
2. Rewrites, Adjustments, and Assignments
3. Property and Sales Taxes
4. Equipment Location Tracking
5. Monthly Accounting Entries

Billing and Collections

A leasing company's main priority is to get the lessee to pay on time. Many delinquency problems are traced to confusion and misunderstandings at the beginning of the lease. I mentioned earlier that it's a good idea to make sure that the lessee is satisfied with the equipment before funding the lease.

Billing and collections function is complex and delicate. A well-designed invoice can reduce customer complaints and mistakes. The invoice should be clearly designed to inform the lessee of the payment amount and due date.

Rewrites, Adjustments, and Assignments

During the collections, lessors want to avoid legal action and equipment repossession if at all possible. Sometimes a lessee with a cash flow problem can be salvaged by rewriting the lease, usually extending the term with lower payments and adding several skip payments during tight cash flow periods. Although management must weigh this increased risk against the cost of legal action, the best decision often is to rewrite.

Another common situation is an adjustment to the lease. This can happen when the lessee decides that he needs additional equipment add-ons and wants to keep them on the same lease.

Assignments can take place when a lessee sells his business or wants to unload his lease for financial reasons. The lessor must monitor this event closely to protect his position, but will usually approve the transaction rather than have to deal with an unwilling lessee. This transaction usually requires a credit check on the new lessee.

Property and Sales Taxes

A subject of increasing concern to lessors is the administrative effort required to properly handle property and sales taxes. And it will probably get more complex after the Streamlined Sales Tax committee issues their final recommendations on taxing transactions over the Internet.

Most states assess personal property taxes to equipment, but they have a wide variety of methods for doing so. This is why multi-regional leasing companies have such a nightmare on their hands.

For example, let's say that a lessor is assessed for all of his equipment leased in Chicago. The lessor declared equipment used by many lessees to make up that equipment group, but the assessor used different formulas for each piece of equipment. The lessor gets the bill and has to break it down in order to re-bill the lessee. When the lessee asks for a copy of the bill as proof, the lessor can only show him the total bill.

Sales and use tax laws vary widely. In many states, cities, counties, and transportation districts, sales tax is assessed on monthly lease rental payments. If a lease has equipment located in several taxing jurisdictions, the lessor must break down the monthly payment by each piece of equipment and assess the pro-rata portion to each lessee.

In some jurisdictions, sales tax is computed on original equipment cost, not the monthly rents. In other cases, some equipment may be exempt due to special taxing authority legislation. This confusion creates a high lessor service cost.

Equipment Location Tracking

To support the complex structure necessary to handle property and sales taxes, a company needs to closely monitor the location of the equipment. This is not an easy task, because the lessor must usually rely on the lessee for this location information. Often the lessor will declare property tax based on his latest information, bill the lessee, and then find out that the lessee has moved the equipment.

Some leasing companies send out confirmation notices to lessees before making the declaration to the taxing authority.

Smart lessors send their equipment management team into the field to check the correct location of the equipment in conjunction with an effective marketing call program.

Monthly Accounting Entries

At the end of every month, accounting entries are booked to the general ledger.

Here are just a few of the monthly entries an Accounting Department makes:

- Lease income
- Fee income
- Depreciation
- Tax Credits
- Debt principal and interest
- Commissions
- Legal and court fees
- Late charge and other miscellaneous revenues

TERMINATION

When a lessor enters into a lease contract, he wants the lessee to perform exactly as the contract stipulates — make each payment on time and exercise the purchase option (unless the lessor intends to re-market the equipment). Any deviations usually reduce lessor profits.

Let's look first at a normal termination.

When the lease nears the end of its term, the lessor sends out a residual invoice to the lessee and encourages him to either renew the lease or purchase the equipment. If the purchase option was fixed at the beginning of the lease, the billing amount is according to the contract. If the purchase amount is fair market value, the lessor must determine the appropriate price.

Lessors negotiate a price with the lessee, encouraging him to retain the equipment. In most cases, the lessor will be successful since the lessee usually doesn't want to replace the equipment if it's providing him an important service. But a shrewd lessee will understand the lessor's position and can often negotiate a lower purchase price or substitute another piece of equipment that he will typically buy through a broker.

When a residual price has been accepted by both parties, the lessee sends a check to the lessor. The lessor formally closes the lease agreement, validates the purchase agreement, passes title to the lessee, prepares accounting close-out entries, and terminates the lease.

If the lease is a short-term rental on an operating lease the lessor may need to arrange for the return of equipment, place it into inventory for re-marketing purposes and begin the process of preparing the asset for resale or re-lease.

Some equipment is sold through auctions on a domestic and international basis depending on the size of the market, the specialty features of the equipment, and the amount of equipment requiring disposition. Some lessors re-lease used equipment for a short period of time and then scrap it.

Buyouts

Occasionally, a lessee will decide that he wishes to purchase the leased equipment before the end of the lease term. In a tax-oriented lease transaction, the lessor must consider the loss from recapturing declared tax benefits. The buyout calculation would be as follows for a direct finance/true-tax lease:

Total net remaining payments

plus

Estimated residual

less
Unearned income

Less

Security deposit

Plus

Billed and un-billed property taxes

Plus

Pre-tax equivalent of recaptured tax credits

Plus

Sales tax on net cash proceeds

This formula often produces a very high purchase price compared to what many lessees expect because they have not considered property taxes, recaptured tax credits and other administrative expenses. Sometimes the lessor may be inclined to negotiate a lower figure to avoid a potential lessee problem, but in doing so will sacrifice profit on the lease.

Upgrades

Upgrades present a slightly different situation. In this case, the lessee is interested in trading in his equipment, usually with the same vendor. The vendor is anxious to accommodate the customer, and since the lessor also wants more business, he is more inclined to discount the value of the old lease.

When an upgrade takes place, the lessor pays the vendor the net cost of the new equipment less the trade-in value of the old.

Non-performance

Despite all efforts to salvage problem accounts, lessors can end up with non-performance leases. Whatever the reason, lessees do not make the monthly payment and becomes delinquent. When all work-out solutions have failed, the lessor must take legal action, or simply write off the account.

Because of the high cost of attorneys and legal proceedings, some accounts are judged to be too small to pursue legally. These accounts generally wind up with a collection agency, which will take at least 50 percent of any amount recovered.

When attorneys do bring legal action, expect to achieve limited results in the short term. Court proceedings take time, and the meter keeps clicking for legal expenses. When all the costs are totaled, a lessor rarely breaks even in a legal situation, even when he wins the court case.

Chapter 7

TWENTY WAYS TO STAND OUT IN A CROWD

Selling is an art not a science. Great salespeople create relationships and breathe life into them. They deliver unique services that create value that cannot be achieved anywhere else in the world. They communicate potential benefits to others without making them feel that they have to give up something to get something. In any words, great salespeople deliver win-win solutions.

Selling requires skills that can be achieved through hard work and dedication to your profession. Your livelihood depends upon your ability to generate enough cash to pay the bills and afford you the lifestyle you want to achieve.

Selling compels you to wake up every day with a great attitude. Selling forces you to listen to other people's problems before you deal with your own. Selling means that you have to find solutions quickly since there are many finance solutions in the marketplace.

If you have a good track history in selling, congratulations. It probably took you a long time to achieve that goal and is probably ingrained in your personality and lifestyle. Making the transition to selling leases may not be as difficult for you as for a person who has great ideas and inventions but has difficulty in selling.

How can you distinguish yourself from the other leading salespeople? Easily. Follow these twenty rules religiously.

1. Show People Who You Really Are

In today's highly competitive environment, clients will only give you a chance if they believe that they will not lose anything as a result of having a relationship with you. They have a fear of sales people and do not want to be your first customer.

Let's face it. You are now a full-time salesperson. You need to sell ideas, solutions, services, products - whatever it takes - to a whole new set of clients. Life will be tough, but you will succeed.

If you display the tangible factors and elements that reflect your personality, you will always feel good about yourself, and your clients will feel good about you, too, coming back for additional services year after year.

2. Professionalize the Outside

Make your resume interesting. Describe who you are and what you can accomplish. It should always be current, fresh, and inviting and should focus on benefits and payoffs that you achieved for other lessees.

Pay special attention to your schooling and knowledge base and highlight unique knowledge that no one else can offer. Give business cards out liberally. They are a very inexpensive form of advertising.

Dress professionally. How you dress reflects your taste and attitude toward success. Dress according to your client's environment and do not spend too much on a brand new wardrobe until cash flow is steady. Arrive on time for clients and never be late. Your client's time is precious and it is a privilege that they grant you.

Always leave extra time between appointments since some customers love to talk. Communicate and write clearly. Ideas, thoughts and actions need to be documented and presented. Always use an automated spell checker, grammar checker, dictionary, and thesaurus before letting any document or presentation out of your sight.

3. Personalize the Inside

Set up an office that reflects you. If you operate out of your home, set up a separate place where you can focus on the business. Decorate your office with things that make you feel good. Hang up pictures of places that you want to go, and paste posters of empowering thoughts where you can see them when you feel down.

Get the best computer that you can afford. It will pay off handsomely with increased productivity. Track potential and existing client relationships, create letters and correspondence, prepare and make presentations, search the Internet and analyze lessee financials.

Set up separate telephone lines for your business. Get two business lines to take phone calls. Often, you will be talking to one client when another client calls. Or you are talking to a client while searching the Internet for information. Avoid having your client get a busy signal or an answering machine.

Get voice mail and a high-speed DSL Internet connection. You cannot beat the price or service for the value received.

4. Build Rapport With Prospects

People either like you or hate you within a few seconds. It has to do with rapport. The best salespeople use rapport to create an environment that is inviting. If the prospect enjoys the environment, there is a high probability that he or she will continue to talk and let you know their needs.

Try these techniques:

- **Show Interest** – *Use a short phrase that lets the prospect know you are right there with him and interested in what he is saying. Phrases such as "That sounds fantastic" or "That's incredible" lets them know you are right there with him. Remember, everyone loves to talk about subjects they care about, and the experience is even more rewarding when the audience is* *enthusiastic as well.*

- **Restate What They Said** — *Think about how comfortable it is to have someone repeat your words back to you. Something like "I can't believe you were just in Paris. I love that city."*

- **Restate The Emotion Behind What They Say** — *Perhaps the most powerful of all three is to capture the emotion behind what the speaker is saying and feed that back to her. Dale Carnegie said that people bristle with prejudices, pride and vanity and that everyone is driven by emotion. To restate the emotion a person is feeling is to capture the essence of communication.*

5. Position for success

Get back to your client by the time and date that you promised. It is your responsibility to manage your lessee since she has no particular loyalty to you and can always change her mind.

You must always demonstrate integrity and consistency. Lessees are always wary of lessors and feel uncomfortable because they need you. Never give them the opportunity to question you by giving them inconsistent facts or opinions. Often, plans do not happen as expected. Flexibility is a major key to success. You must always be able to think quickly, adapt accordingly, and prepare a new set of directions.

Never be afraid to share ideas with a potential lessee. Sometimes, the client checks you out before he buys your service. Sometimes, the client may take your idea and run without you. Nonetheless, sharing ideas with clients will usually solidify the relationship quickly and make it more difficult for your competition to knock you out of the picture.

6. Visualize Your Future

Begin each day by setting goals. Start off with what's important to you in life. To make your goals real, write them down, memorize them and repeat them verbally. Goals need to be reinforced every day. If yesterday's goals are no good, throw them away and create new ones. Visualize all possibilities and dream a little.

Goals need to make sense and need to be specific to your business. Do no waste a lot of energy spending time and thought on concepts that yield no productive output.

Goal setting should be manageable and measurable.

Once a month, write down your accomplishments. Measure them against your goals. See if they are still working. Drop or reorganize goals that take you away from making money. Remember that you need to bring in cash to make ends meet.

Try this 4-step process:

(1) Write down what you want to accomplish between now and the end of your leasing career. If you do not write it down, it will never happen.
(2) Write down your personal goals for the next year. Personal goals may include, family, personal growth, finances, health, social, career, hobbies, spiritual, and recreation.
(3) Go back and compare your first two lists. Make sure that the items on your short-term list will, as you attain them, help you attain your longer term goals.
(4) Review your goals. If there are any that you are not willing to pay the price for, cross them off, leaving only those items you are willing to make happen. Now, on a third sheet of paper, create the job goals that are important to you over the next 12 months.

Identify what outcomes you want to attain or achieve in the next year. Some key areas in which you might consider writing job goals include: leasing sales, accounting, tax, documentation, equipment management, pricing, analysis, management, marketing, personnel, funding, legal, systems and credit.

For each of the three lists, take another sheet of paper and list the activities that you must do to attain your most important goals.

I used this approach when I was terminated from Euromoney. The Executive Vice President of the Division flew over (first class) from London to Salt Lake City.

I knew he hated me, but I thought he respected me. He had e-mailed me three weeks prior telling me that he wanted to have breakfast and discuss the future of the company.

I was excited to see him. When I showed up at the hotel restaurant he had already had breakfast. Not a good sign. After brief trivialities, he handed me a two-page document that indicated I was "too expensive". I was in shock. I told him that I would review the document, which offered me 1099 status, and get back to him.

Dad told me a long time ago: hire the best accountants, lawyers and mechanics to do the job that is needed. I knew that my US lawyer could beat their London lawyer.

After reviewing my choices, I realized that if I was going to become independent, I might as well form my own company. I also realized that they could not enforce my covenant not to complete because it had been drafted too broadly.

When my lawyer asked Euromoney for a detailed list of clients that I could not solicit, they backed off. I can only guess that they could not put together the list in a timely fashion or feared releasing it to me.

7. Weather the Storm

Since December 1, 2000 U.S. employers have announced nearly 2.5 million job cuts. The technology (Nortel, Motorola, Worldcom, Lucent), manufacturing (GE, Honeywell, DaimlerChrysler), Finance (JP Morgan, Aetna, Charles Schwab), Media (Disney, AOL Time Warner, NY Times), Internet (Amazon, Webvan, Yahoo), and Retail (Montgomery Ward, JC Penney, Circuit City) industries have all claimed casualties.

The Big 4 accounting firms have pending lawsuits for issues ranging from bad audit opinions to SEC rules violations. And Arthur Andersen failed due to Enron.

Alan Greenspan continues to fight inflation and keep interest rates low. But the stock market is still in negative territory with more down days than up. Inside traders are net sellers as they jettison their equity shares. And the market is anemic and uneven.

Business behavior can no longer be predicted. No one knows what to do.

Therefore, if you are in the 'selling' profession, you have entered un-chartered waters. Selling leasing has become extremely difficult and painful. Only the most seasoned sales professionals are surviving. Given this market, how can you hold on long enough to weather the storm? You need to look and act the role of a successful sales person before you actually get there.

Many years ago, I lectured in Mexico. A student asked me to review a recent marketing experience. He told me that a potential client threw him out of the office. He told me, that when asked how long he had been in the business, he responded "three weeks." I told him that I would have probably thrown him out as well. What can a "three week rookie" teach me?

To encourage him to go back and try again, I told him that he probably had other work experience that he did not share with the potential client. He told me that he had been a waiter for the last four years. I told him, from now on, to tell people that he had four years of service experience and had been in finance for less than a year.

8. Research

Use Google, AskJeeves or Yahoo as a starting point. There is so much material on the Internet. You can find articles on different subjects, industry contacts, private and public companies, annual reports, credit information, tax returns, financial statements and competitor's intelligence.

9. Read

Read as much as you can. See where the world is going. Look for ideas in books, magazines, and the Internet. In order to expand your brain, you need to stretch it in ways that you have never imagined. Try to see multiple angles and other people's perspectives. Research constantly. Analyze why things happen and identify patterns. If you can predict people's behavior, you can align yourself with most people and develop solutions to meet their needs.

Here are some reading suggestions:

- **Books.** *Study authors such as Tony Robbins, Zig Ziglar, Og Mandino, Richard Bayan, and Stephen Covey. You may not agree with their philosophies, but you will have a better perspective of the selling process and human nature.*

- **Newspapers.** *Learn what is going on with senior management and the companies that are doing well in the current business market. Get a better understanding of the problems that they are experiencing, so that you can help solve them.*

- **Association-produced material**. *They have a very strong interest in keeping their members profitable and in business.*

10. Watch, Look and Listen

Watch how other professionals solve problems. There is no greater thrill than watching a pro. They are rare. How many people ever get to run a Disney, McDonalds or Fedex?

Why should you watch another professional? Why should you copy their style, their words, their approach? Why should you mimic their behavior, their methodology, their game plan? Simply, because it works.

*I am not suggesting that you violate any copyright law, patent rules or governmental regulations that take away their unique advantages. Or copy the behaviors of financial crooks from companies that you see in the **Wall Street Journal** or **Financial Times**. Simply said, create your own unique method of solving problems by adding value that you can call your own.*

Watch and study TV and Internet ads. Although most products may not be useful or appropriate for the leasing business, you may find that similar marketing ideas can be employed to your benefit. Call their toll free numbers and look at the quality of their marketing material. Listen to the sales rep speech. Read the glossy brochures, look at the photographs, analyze ad copy to see what you think will work best for you.

11. Solve problems quickly

Solve problems quickly before they get out of hand. One of my favorite mentors, Tony Robbins, says kill the monster while it is tiny. Deal with the problem now. That way, you will not use up a lot of energy. If you are unhappy, it just means that you are not happy with your current situation and have not yet figured out how to solve the problem. You may have to do more research, talk to more people, attend more meetings, read more material, but you will figure it out. You must stick with it until you make it right.

12. Spend the day productively

Og Mandino, another one of my favorite authors, said you need to live for the day. He said that you cannot change the past nor the future, so why worry about it? Today is the only day you can work with and do something about. I have gone one step further and translated this philosophy into financial language that I can relate to; yesterday is a canceled check and tomorrow is a promissory note. Today is a gift and that is why they call it the present. Your values, experiences and mistakes entitle you to make as much as you want. Take advantage of them and price your value accordingly in the marketplace.

13. Achieve new heights

Reach higher than you have ever reached before. Do not let other people influence you to stop, slow down, or start over, unless you feel that way, too. Remember, there are very few entrepreneurs in the world so probability says that non-entrepreneurs will outnumber you as advisors.

14. Select the best choices

Make your choices carefully. Often, you will face two great opportunities at the same time. Unfortunately, you will have to choose. It will not be easy. Zero in on the choices that will pay you back over time. Plant a lot of trees that will blossom year after year and do small things to cover your basic short-term needs while you are planting the fruits of your future.

15. Accept intellectual opportunities

Take on opportunities that intellectually stimulate you. Go where other people are afraid to go. Look at each opportunity to learn something new. Learn something of value that you can share with other people down the road. Your expertise will pay you handsomely in the long-term.

16. Display good behavior

Be the best in your business. Stick to the highest levels of morality and never treat yourself before honoring your client's needs. Accept your triumphs with dignity. Never believe that you are infallible. Remember, it may have been only days ago that you felt the pain of failure. Your triumphs will be few and far between and there will be periods of no triumphs.

17. Give thanks

Give thanks to all the people who guided you to this point and give thanks to the thoughts in your head that guide you every living day. Allow yourself the opportunity to feel good about what you did, are doing, and will do in your business. Thank each and everyone for the little things that they do for you. You will never know when one small thank you may turn into a great opportunity for your business.

18. Make a list of what you can offer lessees

Write down what you believe are your best skills. Look for a pattern. Determine unique reasons why people should buy from you. Do you have a lower cost than your competitor? Are you more knowledgeable in a particular area? Do you have unique knowledge that you acquired over the years? Are you in a better location than your competitors?

19. Make a list of lessees you want

Make a list of the people or corporations you want to have as clients? Take a few minutes and figure out why they are on your list. Are they prestigious names? Are they close to your office? Do you know people in the company? Is it realistic to get in the doors of a Fortune 100?

Keep the list fresh and update it every week. I try to update my list on Friday afternoons or Saturday mornings when I have the time to think without the distraction of telephones and faxes. Prune the list for deadwood. Add new names to the list in order to have a fresh supply every week. Grow your list at a reasonable rate. Be careful to not add to the list referrals that do not meet your criteria.

20. Make yourself available

Availability is one of the major keys to success. You need to be available literally twenty four hours a day. That does not mean that you need to respond twenty four hours a day. By setting up a good telephone, beeper, cellular, e-mail and fax response system you can always make yourself available to your clients.

Lessees respond more favorably when they believe that you are there for them. They require attention and need to have their problems solved as soon as possible. Selling is the art of responding to their problem quickly, effectively and efficiently.

Follow these twenty rules and I guarantee you will succeed in your career.

Chapter 8

IDENTIFY MARKETING OPPORTUNITIES

There will always be good times and bad times. The best salespeople learn to make the most of the good times and live through the bad times. Ironically, you never know when you are about to begin the next "times". That is why the ability to adjust quickly is so important.

During the tough times, try to avoid these five common mistakes:

COMMON MISTAKES

1.   Push the prospect to buy

You cannot make anyone buy your product. No matter how good you are. You might be able to do it once, maybe twice. But not often enough to make a living at it. People buy when they are ready and they usually sell themselves after you have been able to show them the advantages of dealing with you. Too many people let their egos get in the way. And, they do not know they are proselytizing themselves.

2.   Put down the competition

Many times, a potential prospect is going to ask you about your competition. Never put down your competition. Even if you feel that way. Tell the prospect that they're a good competitor. If you have nothing nice to say, don't say anything. If you say nasty things about your competition your prospect will think that you will talk nasty about them to someone else.

3.   Be insincere

Anyone can compliment another by just saying "Nice tie, great office". It doesn't take much work. And that's why it doesn't work. Add value to your compliment. "Nice tie. Givenchy?" or "Great office, I see you have a spectacular view of the Wasatch Mountains".

4.   Scare them into buying

No one can scare prospects into doing business. You do not nor will you ever have the power to do that. Even if you could, they would hate you for doing it. Putting pressure on another professional doesn't work. Might work in retail. Never in a professional sale.

5.   Forget "two resumes" walked in the door.

For leasing professionals who have just started out, focus on the breadth and depth of your company. For leasing professionals who work for start-ups, focus on the breadth and depth of your own experience. People buy wisdom and experience.

GETTING AN APPOINTMENT WITH A DECISION-MAKER

Timing is everything. Research shows that 20 percent of all prospects are happy with their current situation and most likely will not change. Sixty percent of all prospects are satisfied but will change for the right reason. The remaining 20 percent of all prospects are so fed up with their current situation that they are looking for you while you are looking for them.

I cannot tell you how many times people have taken my class or heard me lecture and said, "I wish I had known you two years ago. I could have really used your lessons then".

Research indicates that you have an 86 percent chance of getting an appointment with a decision-maker if you have someone inside the prospect's organization setting up the meeting. Therefore, you should spend the majority of your prospecting time meeting as many decision-makers or connectors as possible. That is why networking is such a powerful tool.

FIVE STEP SELLING PROCESS

Many salespeople fail because they do not keep enough prospects in the pipeline and therefore do not close enough sales. I have found that this 5-step process ensures success.

Step One: Initiate

Anytime you initiate a new contact you need to answer the following 5 W's - what, when, who, where and why. If you cannot answer all 5 W's then you need to either do more homework or drop this prospect.

Let's look at the following sentence:

I sell customized lease and loan products, at a profit, to decision-making clients who have the money to pay me.

What?	*Sell Lease/Loan Products*
When?	*Use Budgets*
Who?	*Identify Decision Makers*
Where?	*Find Profitable Territories*
Why?	*Meet Client Needs*

Remember that you can offer your clients both leases (operating leases) and loans (finance leases) or other financial products (leveraged leases, synthetics leases, munis, etc).

If the client does not have the budget, determine when the money will be available (deferred leases, skip leases).

If the person you are dealing with is not the decision-maker, find out who is. Many people will lie to you and waste your time. I call them shoppers and stoppers. I think they lie because they are either embarrassed or enjoy playing with vendors. In either case, it is their problem, not mine.

Anyone can give away or substantially discount a product/service to win the business. I see it all the time. It takes perseverance and talent to prove to your client that your product is worth more and is priced accordingly.

Finally, clients want a product that meets their needs. Leasing is a flexible product and is perfect for the client who wants specific options built into the contract.

Step Two: Present

Leasing is sold to both functional (users) and technical (systems) professionals and paid for by finance (accountants). You have to be able to present your credentials to more than one party and tailor your message. In other words, based on the situation, you have to be able to act differently.

First, leasing solves problems. Develop a mutual understanding of the problem to be solved, such as how can I acquire $2 million worth of computers for $1 million? Or, how do I plow the field in half the time since I cannot afford to hire good farm hands? Or, what can I do to increase sales without increasing overtime?

Second, get both technical and functional people to agree on your suggested strategy. If either party disagrees with you, you probably cannot win the business. The functional people will use the equipment that you are financing, but the technical people need to buy in. Otherwise, they may suggest another technical path that may not require any financing.

Third, learn the purchasing process. Find out who writes the check. Find out who evaluates the solution. In the largest companies, neither the functional nor the technical people do the lease vs. buy analysis or issue the purchase order.

Fourth, present your company and your personal credentials. As I mentioned earlier, always focus on your strengths, whether it be the company or you personally. If you focus on both, you have a winner. The only thing that may stop you are the terms and conditions contained in the leasing contract.

Finally, build momentum and certainty. Very few sales go quickly. Most of them take time. Therefore, during each meeting, make sure you book another meeting and agree to next steps. Without a clear path, the transaction will probably die in process, wasting your time. Always ask the prospect for permission to proceed to the next step. If they do not grant it, handle the objection or put it on the back burner for a slow cook.

Step Three: Qualify

- ### Sense of Urgency

If there is no sense of urgency, there is no sale. Think of your own experiences. Think about the holidays, end of quarter, time-limited special offers. We make our buying decisions when the pressure is on. Think about redoing a kitchen, a car that is leaking oil, a faucet that drips. We look when we want, but we buy when we need.

- ### Essential use of the asset

If the lessee really does not need the asset, they will not pay their bills. Think about a municipality. They have to have their police cars, fire trucks and ambulances. Do they really need their golf courses and copiers? Think about a major airline. Do they really need another airplane?

Unfortunately, many of us will lease an airplane to a major airline because we think it is cool! Nonetheless, the day will come when the company may not be able to pay their bills (i.e. Pan American, Western, Vanguard, US Air, National, etc.) and we look back and wonder what went wrong. Nothing went wrong. Simply, they never needed the asset.

- ### Prior leasing experience

Positive experience is good. We just have to be better. Find out what the lessee did not like with the other leasing experience. Negative experience is also good. We can correct their bad experiences. Neutral experience or no experience is bad. There is no emotion to hook onto.

- ### Is it in the budget?

No matter how much a potential lessee likes you, if they do not have the money there is nothing you can do about it. Companies put money into either capital budgets (intend to pay cash or finance) or operating budgets (intend to rent or lease). You need to know if they have already budgeted for the acquisition or is it just a dream.

Step Four: Demonstrate

- ### Write original and sincere letters

I receive hundreds of form letters and solicitations, via mail and Internet, daily. At this point in my career, I can usually spot them. They start with Mr. Taylor (my name is Jeffrey) or sir or colleague or resident or some other phrase that does not make me want to look. If you are going to solicit me, you have to get my attention. Form letters do not work for experienced, senior professionals. We have seen too much carbon copy to even pay attention.

- ### Give referrals

Even though I have been in the business for more than 20 years, I am still asked for referrals. I am reminded of Barbra Streisand, who at the height of her career, told an audience that she still had to audition for her roles. Therefore, I give referrals. But, I first ask clients for their permission. I've learned that many people from whom I might anticipate a glowing referral have gone on in their careers, left the leasing industry – or died. Always call your referrals first. There is nothing worse than giving out a useless referral and leading the prospect to a dead end.

- ### Use client's info in your presentation

The Internet has made it easy to find out a lot about your prospective client before you make your pitch. You can study their background, their niche, how Wall Street views them, what investors think about the company, what the press thinks, what the major manufacturing associations think, etc. If you do your homework, you can incorporate your potential client's logos, head shots, and numbers into tightly-knit presentations that will impress.

- ***Use statistics to reinforce your position***

I love statistics. Presented properly, they not only impress, they convince. You can look to the government (bls.gov), SEC (edgar.com), major leasing associations (elaonline.com), US press (wsj.com), foreign press (ft.com), and newswires (prnewswire.com) to get a feeling on how the rest of the world feels about your prospect and her industry.

- ***Customize product offerings***

Every lessee wants to feel important and be treated with the utmost respect. Customize your documentation, terms and conditions, payment schedules, early termination options, and upgrade options to create a unique product that stands out in the crowd.

Step Five: Close

I love closing. I think it takes a lot of courage to ask someone for business. I remember starting out in sales and found it very difficult to close. I did not think I deserved the business. Then I met another sales professional who said that you were doing a disservice to a potential client if you did not ask for the business. Especially, if you had a product or service that they could use.

I like verbal closings because the risk is limited. Think of it as a formal close without the documentation. I like the "assumptive" close. It uses the word "if". For example, "If we can get the parties to agree on Paragraph 8, do we have a deal?" or "If I can get management to offer you an extra 6-months extended warranty, are you ready to sign?"

I like this technique because the brain cannot hear the word "if". It is too small. Under pressure, the brain optimizes words and hears "We can get the parties to agree..." or "I can get management to offer..."

If you don't believe me try using the word if, and, or of in any search engine in the world. All of them will say the words if, and, or of have been ignored.

- **Get the signature**

Have the potential lessee sign a letter of intent. Before you do additional documentation you can minimize your risk by getting them to sign a letter that basically says you can proceed. I have found that this simple act allows me to watch their real feelings. If signing a letter to proceed is difficult and they ask a lot of questions, you can rest assured that getting them to sign a formal contract is going to be worse.

- **Draft terms and conditions**

With the advent of computers, word processors, lasers, EDI, fax and the Internet, the process of drafting terms and conditions has become a lot easier. However, with lessees demanding flexibility and their desire to show contracts to their accounting and legal teams, you can expect to rewrite the contract a couple of times before everyone feels satisfied.

- **Get all decision makers involved**

Previously, I said that there are three decision makers — users, systems, and accountants/finance. If you do not keep all three decision makers in the loop, you are giving your competitors an opening that could quickly turn into a lost sale.

- **Reinforce the fact that they are making a good decision**

Lessees want to know that they are making a good decision. They need to hear it from someone they trust – you. Here's an example:

The next time you go to a fine restaurant, listen intently to your server. He has been professionally trained to make your experience as enjoyable as possible.

For example, let's say that they are offering specials that evening. After the choice of water routine (bottled water or tap) he will probably use a "perception of choice" close such as "Would you like to order off the regular menu or hear our specials?" The perception of choice close uses the word "or".

When you get to the point of ordering your meal, listen to his response.

Nine out of ten times, if you order one of the most expensive meals, they will respond with "excellent choice". This technique reinforces the fact that you made a wise decision, thus minimizing your backing off and choosing something less expensive.

NEVER BE LIED TO AGAIN

There is a gentleman in Long Island named David Lieberman. He is a Ph.D. and an expert in gaining confessions from criminals. In his book, Never Be Lied To Again he analyzes how criminals think, act and respond to pressure.

Although they are not criminals, some lessees present behaviors that may indicate potential problems that need to be dealt with quickly before they become more difficult. Here are some of Lieberman's observations that I believe apply to lessees.

- *Guilty people stall and do not like to make decisions*
- *People who lie tend to make simple things difficult*
- *People who lie react quickly and emotionally to perceived threats*
- *People who lie have difficulty saying no - they do not return phone calls and do not respect most people*
- *They tend to repeat your questions*

So, the next time, you meet someone who is expressing one or more of these conditions, put up your shield.

In summary, the best salespeople identify their targets before pursuing potential customers. They recognize that they need to:

- *Avoid common mistakes when they are in the presence of a prospect.*
- *Keep a lot of qualified customers in the pipeline.*
- *Drop prospects who are wasting their time.*

Follow these rules and you will find that you will have more time available to go after better, higher paying lessees.

Chapter 9

EIGHTEEN WAYS TO WIN MORE BUSINESS!

In today's selling environment, people tend to not grant a marketing call to a beginner. They are already served by many companies and adding another lessor to the mix requires a detailed strategy. Specifically, the leasing salesperson has to find a niche within the lessee organization that answers the question: What is my competitor not providing the lessee?

I have found through many years of training sales professionals that if you prepare for a marketing call, you can not only get the appointment but get the business as well.

First, remember that there are five essential human behaviors, which influence any financing decision.

- **People buy with emotion and justify it with logic**

Professionals do not look for cheap solutions. They look for solutions that are commensurate with their life style. If people always bought on price, then everyone would own a KIA or a Volkswagen instead of a Mercedes.

Successful salespeople determine which emotional factors sway their customers into leasing. Most lessees will pay more for a lease than a loan, if they see value in the transaction. They will then justify the higher price with logic, in order to defend their position to senior management or partners.

- **The one with the most powerful belief wins**

There is no concept called truth. There are only beliefs. As a result, in any negotiation, the party with the strongest belief wins. If a customer does not buy from you, it only means that her negative belief outweighs your positive belief. Beliefs can be changed. You just have to work at changing them.

- ***Everybody knows somebody***

Never walk away empty-handed. If a potential client does not see the need to do business with you, he may still give you some great referrals. Guilt works wonders.

- ***Clients need your help***

Go in with the attitude that everyone needs your help. If it they do not see it, it does not matter. As long as you keep trying, they will eventually come around. Sometimes it may take a minute, an hour, a day, or longer than that. Stay in the battle as long as you feel good about it.

- ***No one wants you to fail***

The world is littered with people who wanted to make it big. Some made it and then lost it. Others tried and never made it. Regardless of where you are at this moment in time, take a deep breath, and say to yourself, "No one wants me to fail".

Now that you are armed with the knowledge that people buy with emotion and justify it with logic, we can now explore specific tactics to carry out your mission — finding great prospects who will find that you and your company are a notch above the rest.

1. Do not compete on price

Assume that your organization does not have the lowest cost of capital. If a lessee wants a cheap solution, they are probably going to go somewhere else. I know of no way to distinguish yourself, based on price. Your rates need to be competitive and within 200 basis points of the nearest competitor, but you do not have to be cheap. People buy value.

2. Never use the "L" word in a presentation

Some lessees hate leasing because another lessor burnt them. Some lessees do not understand leasing since they have never leased before. Other potential lessees have heard bad things about leasing and do not trust the product. It does not make sense to use a word that might be misconstrued or interpreted poorly. Use the word finance. This way you will have the opportunity to offer finance leases (disguised loans) or tax leases. Either way you win more business.

3. Figure out a way to do the deal

Attitude is everything. An organization must find a way to do the deal. If the customer is talking to you, they are interested in doing business with you. Some of them may be shopping the deal, others might be getting rate quotes and setting you up. Most of them want the best deal and the lowest possible price. If you are more expensive, your client needs a way to justify the higher price. Give them a creative solution that is unique and stands out from the rest.

4. Dig deeper

Most of the great credits are already happy. Even if you have a superior product and wonderful personality, they will not change. Change requires a lot of effort, and most finance professionals have more pressing needs. Try digging deeper. Go after clients who are considering leasing for the first time. There are a lot of companies climbing their way up who need your help. They just do not know that you are there. Go find them.

5. Go back to basics

Leasing products (i.e. synthetic leases, leveraged leases, deferred equity leases, venture leases) have become extremely complex. A lot of our clients have a general distrust toward the leasing product. Find out the essential benefits of your product and stop focusing on the technical structure. Show the client how to turn on the light and not how to create electricity.

6. Change your habits

If you do not know where you are going, any path will take you there. If you want to get somewhere in particular you need to focus on changing your current habits. Some people need to make more phone calls. Others need to learn how to write more effectively. Some need to develop better communication skills. Whatever you do, listen to people who know how to help you.

7. Learn the common objections

Some lessees do not want to talk. They throw Teflon statements at you like, "I don't understand leasing", " all leasing companies look alike" and "we are unique". At that moment, there is nothing you can say to make things right. It is better to reschedule the meeting and move on to a different setting.

Other lessees hide their feelings with statements like "leasing takes too long", "your rates are too high" and "your residual assumptions are too low." Simply answer "compared to what?" and let them continue to talk. Let them fill you in on where they are coming from before you respond.

Some objections require lessors to change documents or options. Respond with the word "if". For example, if the potential lessee says, "I want to be able to cancel at will". You respond, "if we can show you how to cancel at will, do we have a deal?". But, please make sure that you have the authority to take it to the next level. Worse case, you can always say, "I can't promise anything. Let me see what I can do."

8. Remind yourself that you are number one

People in first place do not look at the behavior of the number twos and threes. It is wasted energy and does not change the battlefield. Focus on getting and keeping the client. Innovation comes from within; not from copying another competitor. Don't look at the people behind you. When you are running a race, you do not have the luxury to stop and look back. Those precious seconds (basis points in our business) can cost you the race. Do not fear the contender behind you. Remember their view is a lot different than yours. Remember the lead dog in the dog sled. All others see someone else's rear.

9. **Walk through hell**

Many sales professionals do not realize that they need to go through a period of hellish growth. You will have to work abnormal amounts in short periods of time. Trust me when I say this. Heaven is at the end. But it is hell getting there.

10. **Respect others**

You cannot get to first place by yourself. You need a support team. You only have your own energies to give, and that is not enough. Each of the players plays a role on the team of success. Accounting works the numbers, tax minimizes tax, and asset management gets more out of the residual. There can be no weak links on the team or the lessee is going to go somewhere else on the next deal.

11. **Create new ideas**

You need to create new ideas to become and remain a leader. There is always someone out there who wants to take your place. If you run out of ideas, it's time to go on vacation, take a break, go back into the classroom. You need to reenergize your brain from time to time.

12. **Do not give credence to the enemy**

If you pay attention to the enemy, you give them credence. The worst insult in the world is to ignore someone. You cannot worry about what your competitor may or may not do. Don't waste your time about something you cannot change.

13. **Be persistent until they say no**

If lessees talk to you, they want to do business. The fact that they tell you what another competitor offers them means that they would prefer to do business with you. Otherwise, they are wasting both their time and yours. Until they say no, you can win the business.

14. Develop relationships

It is a lot easier to sell an existing client a new product than to develop a new client from scratch. If the relationship works, develop it. Talk to your favorite lessees and find out how you can help them. Offer them advice from time to time. Show that you care. You'll be surprised by how much new information can be turned into profitable business.

15. Balance your personal life

Never throw away the balance in your life. You need a lot of personal satisfaction to maintain a strong business race. Excellent diet and exercise are also important. If you destroy yourself to achieve business success, then your success cannot endure. You cannot take it with you, so don't try.

16. Kiss a lot of toads along the way

Be friendly with people you do not like. Close your eyes and kiss a frog. If nothing happens, kiss another frog. Someday, you will open your eyes and find out your best customer (and friend) started out as a frog.

17. Apologize for other's mistakes

Sooner or later, you'll have to deal with a difficult customer. Many are picky, know-it-alls, egocentrics, fault-finders, and constant complainers. Unfortunately, too many leasing professionals, when faced with hostile lessees, choose to avoid the situation.

This results in one of two things happening: Either the angry client decides the problem isn't worth the aggravation and cools down. Or the client gets so angry that she shares her displeasure with your company's higher-ups, who then absorb some of the client's anger and all too happily deliver it to you.

18. Show Patience

You must show patience with everyone. If you feel you are losing your patience, go out and get yourself a cookie and take 15 minutes to eat it. You will be amazed how calming a warm chocolate cookie feels in the midst of tension.

Naturally, no one wants to walk into a lion's den and face the angry client. However, you must consider the value of this client to you, your reputation, and the company. In most cases, it is worth your while to face that angry customer and get the situation resolved as quickly as possible.

With all of the problems you will face in the leasing industry, your worst nightmare will be the angry lessee or vendor. In many cases, they feel that they have been wronged and will complain until you do something about it.

Research indicates that customers who complain are likely to continue doing business with your company if they feel that they were treated properly.

It's estimated that as many as 90 percent of customers who perceive themselves as having been wronged never complain — they just take their business elsewhere. So if they are still talking to you, they are saying that they want to save the relationship. So, how do you handle an angry, complaining customer? Let's begin with a couple of tools you can use in these situations.

- **RESPECT** - *It is difficult to respect a person who yells, swears and behaves like an infant. Keep in mind that you are not the object of the customer's anger. Since you are in control, and they are not, you can help him with his problem.*

- **EMPATHY** - *Put yourself in the client's shoes. Try to see the situation from her perspective. Don't try and cut her off. Listen carefully. If someone is angry or upset, it is because that person feels injured in some way. The best salespeople let the customer vent and try to understand the source of that frustration. Try this line the next time a lessee or vendor yells at you:*

"It sounds like something has gone wrong, and I can understand your frustration. I'm sorry you're experiencing this problem. Let's take a look at the next step."

- **IDENTIFY THE PROBLEM** - *Sometimes while the angry customer is venting, you'll be able to latch right on to the problem because it's clear-cut. Something is broken. Or late. Or the client thinks a promise has been broken. Ask the client to give you details. These kind of questions force the customer to think about facts instead of his feelings about those facts. So, you interject a more rational kind of conversation.*

- **APOLOGIZE** - *Now that he is listening, you can apologize. Some people believe that an apology is an acknowledgment of wrongdoing. But you can appreciate and apologize for the customer's inconvenience without pointing fingers. And, above all, avoid blame.*

- **AVOID BLAME** - *Don't blame the customer by saying something like **"Are you sure you understood the monthly rent quote?"** This will ignite his anger all over again because you are questioning his credibility and truth-telling. And don't blame your company or your vendor by saying, **"I'm not surprised your invoice was wrong. It's been happening a lot."***

- **RESOLVE THE PROBLEM** – *Since you may not have the power or authority to fix the problem, you may need to buy yourself some time. It's critical to leave the irate lessee or vendor with the understanding that your goal is to resolve the problem. You may need to say, **"I'm going to need to make some phone calls."** If you do, give the customer an idea of when you'll get back to him. And remind him that you appreciate his patience and that you will work hard to get things fixed.*

The bottom line is you can learn specific techniques and tactics to generate and win new business. But I have always felt that my best relationships required me to turn around difficult situations. And those are the ones that lasted the longest and enriched both of us.

Welcome to the Leasing Industry!
Next Chapter: Work the Network

Chapter 10

WORK THE NETWORK

You need to invest in yourself. Many leasing companies have cut back on improving intellectual capital over the last 10 years. In order to keep up or, better yet, improve your marketable skills, you need to constantly get more education.

Your education will come in many different formats, styles and sources. Some education will be good, some will be bad. Some education will be free, some expensive. Your education will include formal classroom training as well as informal hallway discussions. All education has value. It teaches you what to do or not to do under varying circumstances.

Where are you going to go for this education? There are so many sources that it is impossible to list them all.

For example,

- *What magazines, journals, newspapers should you read?*
- *Should you buy them at a newsstand, subscribe to them, or read them at the library?*
- *What courses should you take? Should you take one-shot classes through a professional organization or take courses over a semester at the local college?*
- *Should you buy self-help books? Which ones should you purchase? Should they be technical in nature or more psychological?*
- *What software training do you need? Which technical platforms will survive as the mainstream of the future? Which Internet providers will give you the most bang for the buck? Will they be around next year?*

- *What kind of financial budget do you need to establish?*
- *Should you borrow money, get a part time job to supplement your entrepreneurial efforts, or take money from the savings account?*

I have had some of my greatest educational experiences when I have had to take out my credit card and roll the dice. I can honestly say that the dividends were fabulous and that I would not have done anything differently now that I have the fortune of hindsight.

Join Networking Groups

I know of no better way to get educated than to join networking groups. A networking group is designed to foster business relationships among entrepreneurs. They are usually supported by Chambers of Commerce or professional societies who have members such as accountants, lawyers, advertising professionals, builders and lenders.

Networking among professionals can be disenchanting at first. They do not open their arms and await your arrival. You have to work hard at meeting people, and it may take months before they recognize you as a regular. This forum is not designed for the quick and easy hit.

Networking groups tend to meet after hours since most entrepreneurs need to work during the day. Sometimes there will be luncheon meetings that will include a guest speaker. You can learn a lot from a guest speaker, but don't stop there. Line up a guest-speaking engagement for yourself, and you will have scored a major coup for your business.

Networking groups are also a unique forum to discuss business problems. Face it, most entrepreneurs admire other entrepreneurs and are usually very happy to help out a fellow traveler. The connections that you will make will last a lifetime and can be extremely helpful if you are also interested in rising in local politics.

Joining a networking group is a responsibility. Although it may never directly land you business, it is a strong forum to learn new skills, make new contacts, get new ideas, and provide you with quality referrals.

Some organizations will not let you join unless you are asked by two-three current members. These organizations select members based on how well you may fit into their organization. They will select you based on your business history, personality, prior charitable performance, and leadership skills. Examples include Rotary, Lions, MENSA and religious affiliates.

Other organizations require you to hold a professional degree in the members' fields. Examples include the American Bar Association, American Institute of CPA's and the American Banking Association.

Finding organizations is not difficult. You can talk to neighbors, look in the local newspapers for meeting schedules, and ask other entrepreneurs in your building.

Before you join an organization, go to as many meetings as you deem necessary in order to feel comfortable and better understand the environment. Sit with and talk to as many people as you can. Learn about their philosophies and their expectations about you. Feel free to ask lots of questions since your decision is going to have a major impact on your time and money.

Find out the following:

1. PURPOSE/OBJECTIVE

- What do you want to get out of the group?
- Is it more important to make friends, learn new ideas, or get business?

2. QUALIFICATIONS

- What do you bring to the table?
- Do you have specific knowledge or experience that will help other members?
- Are your credentials satisfactory?
- Do they encourage women to join?
- Do they encourage minorities to join?
- Do they encourage members from government to join?

- *What is the typical member age?*
- *Are they looking for younger people?*

3. LOCATION

- *Where do they meet?*
- *How far away is the meeting place from your office?*
- *Do they change the meeting place to encourage people from different parts of town to attend?*

4. FINANCIAL/TIME OBLIGATIONS

- *How much are the dues?*
- *Are there special rates for commissioned professionals?*
- *Are there special assessments?*
- *Are there special events?*
- *How often do they meet?*
- *What additional time commitments do you need to make outside of the regularly scheduled meetings, such as for special events?*

5. PRIVILEGES

- *Will you feel proud in joining this group?*
- *Will you feel good if they publish your name in their newspaper?*
- *Does your membership include discounts at other establishments?*

Learn to Write Better

Writing good articles is essential to success. No other person knows your unique niche better than you do. The quality of your writing will help you secure business with more upscale lessees.

One book, in particular, had a major impact on my ability to write. It is called Words That Sell by Richard Bayan. Bayan was a copywriter for many years. Over those years, he kept a notebook of words and phrases that helped him when he needed guidance. In his book, he identifies words, phrases, and slogans that he has found worked well in copy that he and his competitors created for clients.

He believes that you need to open with a grabber, something that gets people's attention. Follow up with a description and benefit of the product or service. Clinch the potential client with words that push them toward a decision.

Words are used everywhere in the leasing world. Words are used in business plans, marketing plans, proposal letters, commitment letters, master leases, marketing brochures, monthly newsletters, mid-term upgrades, and end-of-term buyout options, to name a few.

I had a great professor who told me that I should forget what I learned about writing in elementary school. He told me that most people learn how to write in 3rd or 4th grade and never relearn as adults. As children, we are told to say the same thing over and over again in order to develop vocabulary. As adults, your goal is to communicate good thought.

Complex thoughts impress no one. Compound sentences and the use of gerunds, dangling modifiers and misplaced subjects thoroughly confuse the average business person. There is no need to be complex. Some people think complexity allows them to look superior and, therefore, generate more fees.

Superior work comes from the simple fact that you want your audience to understand what you are saying in the shortest amount of time. Time is precious and valuable.

Business writing is nothing like creative writing. Business writing does not entertain like creative writing. That does not mean that it needs to be dull and boring. It still needs to communicate an idea, thought, process, pattern, or objective to an audience. A good course should teach you how to effectively use business grammar, punctuation, and action-oriented messages.

Once you have taken a course, look back at your prior work. Look for the flaws. See how it can be improved, and you will be amazed at how easy it may be to take your original material and improve upon it. You will also see how other lessees may have viewed your work and discover why you did not get or retain them.

Your greatest source of ideas and words will come from other people who have already achieved success as professional writers. Use their ideas and structures. Use their form and tone of voice. Use their style until you create your own unique style. Copying other's styles is flattery, but be extremely careful not to plagiarize other's material. Be liberal in quoting sources and give credit to those who deserve it.

Welcome to the Leasing Industry!
Next Chapter: When You Feel Like Quitting

Chapter 11

WHEN YOU FEEL LIKE QUITTING

Whether you are in leasing sales for the first time or a seasoned veteran, you will periodically feel like giving up. Before you give up your dream, ask yourself the following questions:

- *Why did I want to go into leasing sales in the first place?*
- *Can I change certain things for the better?*
- *Who needs me and can use my services?*
- *What skills do I have that can be marketed at a profit?*
- *How have I helped other lessees?*

If you look at all the alternatives to leasing sales and don't like any of them, it tells you that your personality, drive, ambition, lifestyle and motivation are perfect for leasing.

It says that you like to be in control - to get up when you want, to work when you feel the need, to choose the people you want to do business with, to work in a volatile market. And there are very few professions that can provide you with the mechanism to achieve these desires.

You may feel like quitting because clients are getting to you. Until the client says no you still have the opportunity to forge a solution. The fact that clients may not be answering your letters or telephone calls may only mean that they are too busy with other problems. You may need to telegram them, send them an unusual gift, visit their office, or go higher up in the decision-making ranks.

Persistence is a requirement. You need to hang in there if you believe that the client will benefit from you, your service and your product. You must believe that they are disadvantaged by not taking you seriously.

Just because you do not find enough lessees this month or last, does not mean than you need to give up the business. No matter how old you get or successful you become, you will feel, from time to time, that you want to quit. When you feel this way, ask yourself the following questions:

- *What would I do if I gave up the leasing business?*
- *Who would I have to convince to hire me?*
- *Is this the same thing as selling?*
- *If I have to sell anyway then shouldn't I stay in the leasing business?*

In college we learned something called the sophomoric philosophy. It went something like this. The more you study, the more you know. The more you know, the more you forget. The more you forget, the less you know, so why study?

The corollary goes as follows. The less you study, the less you know. The less you know, the less you forget. The less you forget, the more you know, so why study?

The bottom line is, you need to study to learn your craft well. Selling is acting. But it is real. It is your life and you can make a difference in someone else's life. The fact that you may make money in the process is the reward for your own individual efforts. Do it with passion. And, if you do not feel like selling right now, then lie down and wait until the feeling passes over. Selling was your decision. So take that responsibility seriously and enjoy it.

Sometimes, you will feel like quitting when you can't find enough prospects. When you start to feel bad about yourself, it will show to the rest of the world. Therefore, when things are not going well for you, it may be time to look at the words and style you use in talking to prospects. In other words, you may need to look at your pitch.

- **Perfect Your Pitch**

Your pitch must be better than other professionals if you want to succeed. It is extremely important to budget enough time and energy to critique your pitch.

You will need to critique your pitch several times. You will first need to critique your pitch after you have come up with the idea. Since your first draft only represents your initial ideas, it will contain flaws and may be perceived as illogical.

Your initial critique must be gentle. You do not want to discourage yourself from finding a more successful pitch. Your second and later critiques must instill perfection in the delivery. These critical sessions should be designed to identify and destroy any flaws.

Too often, leasing professionals do not see how lessees see their pitch. They believe that their pitch is unique, perfect, seamless, clear and intelligible, only to find out that others do not see it the same way.

To critique one's pitch is not easy. You have to literally put your words aside, leave them alone and come back to them with an unbiased, fresh viewpoint, which is next to impossible. But, with hard work and training, it can be done.

- **Maneuver until you get it right**

Within the first 180 days, you may find that you are unhappy with your results. You may be frustrated that you are getting too much negative feedback and not enough clients. Pressure may build up and you may start to question your decision to go into sales.

That is OK. Remember that your dream of going into leasing sales may still be a good decision and that it may be the execution of the plan that needs to be modified. What typically is happening is that, for the first time, you are getting realistic feedback about your strategy and your approach. Instead of taking it personally and telling the world that they are wrong, listen to what they are saying. Maneuver to a new position and modify your strategy to take advantage of this new knowledge. By doing so you will take your business to the position you originally wanted. The only thing you have changed is the way the marketplace perceives you.

- ### *Figure out what is not working*

It is rare that an entire strategy does not work. Usually, it is components of the strategy that do not work and, therefore, weaken the overall strategy. Think of it as a car that is giving you trouble. Fix the brakes or flush the oil before you go out and buy yourself a new car.

Look at you strategy from many different angles. Ask for feedback from people you can trust. Find the weakness that comes up over and over again and replace it. Adapt the strategy and try it. Analyze the restructured strategy in 60 days. Give it time to sink in.

- ### *East is not West*

You will find that a strategy may not work in one place but will work in another. Try out your strategies with more than one person in more than one part of the country. Do not discard a strategy until it has failed in every circumstance. Finding a winning strategy is precious so never let it go.

- ### *Do not change too quickly or too often*

Clients love stability and a predictable lessor. They cannot afford to deal with a person who appears to be everything to everybody or nothing to nobody. Be careful to show the reason for change. If you change too quickly, people will never get to really know you. They will think that you are acting a part and not real or that you cannot be trusted.

- ### *Rework former prospects*

Through good work, you can change subtly and create a new reason for people to do business with you. For example, you may have recently done work for one company and now can use this knowledge in another company that has previously turned you down. Give the old company a new reason to deal with you. Call up some of your former turndowns and rework them. They already know you. And may do business with you this time.

- **Avoid Big Mistakes**

Sometimes, you will feel like quitting because you just brought in a bunch of lousy deals. Again, you didn't do your homework. Forcing issues early in the game will make you more money by closing sales sooner but it can cost you dearly in the long-term. Check out these indicators.

1. Is the lessee moving too quickly?

    Speed often indicates that they may be trying to get you emotionally charged to the point that you lose objectivity. This technique is designed to win your heart and cause you to forget your basic business instincts. It is designed to make you think that you need to move quickly or you may lose the opportunity to get the client's business or the vendor's best price. In fact, an artificial deadline may force you to make a decision before you are ready to accept the risk of that decision. Sales-oriented people will often use this technique especially at month-end or year-end when quotas need to be met.

2. How is the lessee's credit history?

    Less than a clean credit history indicates that they have not paid their bills in the past. Although there may be good explanations, you may be the next person on their list to not get paid. Even if you do good work, and they appreciate it, funds need to be available to honor your invoices. Start up companies usually lack funds and they will cut corners to grow their businesses. Getting a credit report on a client or vendor is easy and inexpensive. Spend the time and do your homework. Do not be persuaded by the prestigious name or reputation of the company. Get the credit report and think of it as a small insurance policy.

3. How good are their references?

    Some clients and vendors do not want to disclose their references due for reasons of privacy. I understand the concept and have been there before. However, I cannot encourage you to take on a client or deal with a vendor who cannot give *you at least one solid reference. There is always some way to get a reference without contradicting or violating the terms and conditions of a non-disclosure agreement. Have the client or vendor show you a contract, letter or correspondence with their reference, after they have whited-out the sensitive parts.*

Some clients and vendors will get incensed that you want to check them out. You have to decide if they are concealing a major fact and hiding something that they do not want you to see. Find out who they do business with. Ask yourself a key question, do you want to get involved with a company that has these types of references?

4. *Where are they located?*

    Just as they are going to check out your office and lifestyle, you will need to do the same. As you get more experienced in your business, you will learn how to detect potential problems more quickly. You will never have a perfect record, but you can learn to improve your batting average.

5. *Are you waking up in the middle of the night?*

    The subconscious mind is absolutely incredible. It warns us when things are not going well. Pay attention to changes in your behavior, sleep patterns, eating habits and attitude. These signs tell you that something is wrong. It is up to you, however, to link it to the client or situation that may be causing the problem.

6. *Is your client sincere?*

    Clients who are going to hurt you appear to be sincere at first. They look positive and act as if you are helping them. They will smile and say all of the right things. As things begin to deteriorate, they will change their attitude and become less sincere. They will start to blame you for your work, find fault with very minute details, and use these faults to set you up for the big kill.

7. *Do they return your phone calls and emails?*

Clients love to avoid problems. Especially, if they think you are the problem. They will not answer phone calls, instruct their secretaries to always say they're in a meeting when you call, fail to respond to your faxes or FedEx letters. Unless you are at the collection level, back off. It is not worth the aggravation or heartache.

In summary, no one can stop you from quitting. And, if that is what you want to do, then do it. But, before you quit, figure out if the "unknown" looks better than the "known." If the "known" looks better, then you know you need to change a lot of things in your life and get back on track.

Chapter 12

ADVANCED MARKETING CONCEPTS

So far, I have helped you learn many techniques on how to improve your performance as a leasing professional. Throughout the previous chapters, I have tried to lay the groundwork on how to do your homework and close more sales.

In this chapter, I am going to focus on some advanced marketing concepts that all of the best salespeople use at one point or another.

Let's start with a credo that you should recite every morning before you go to work.

Pursuing potential customers over and over again in order to complete sales is a constant of selling that never fluctuates. Perseverance is the only way one becomes successful.

Since a leasing contract is an intangible, the best salespeople sell leasing for its benefits. For clients to see benefits they must visualize and believe that leasing gets them to one of the following positions:

- *A desired result*
- *A measurable improvement over existing conditions*
- *Added value (getting more than they paid for)*
- *A gain in a desired direction*
- *A ROI that exceeds expectation*
- *Progress that leads to new opportunities*

You can sell your services to anyone. Since you have to make choices, try to go to the most senior person in the organization. Although it is extremely difficult to get an appointment with a Chairman or President, I have found that if they are interested in what you are selling, they will tell you the truth (sometimes brutally) and they will open the right doors for you.

Finding the Right Match

If you are honest, you cannot convince a potential lessee that your lease has value unless you believe in it yourself. If you don't believe that leasing is the best product in the world, then how can you convince people to take one out?

Can you fake sincerity? In the short-term, yes. In the long-term, no. Board chairmen, Presidents, Chief Financial Officers and all of the other top lessees have an uncanny ability to spot a skunk.

Yet, even if you are the most honest person in the world, you still need to find prospects who can afford you.

- *Do you know what makes a good customer for your company?*
- *Do you do better with public or private companies?*
- *Which industries do you know well?*
- *Will your company fund tough credits?*
- *How long does the lessee have to have been in business?*
- *Where are your lessees located?*

If you know your company well, then you should know where your pricing is vis-à-vis the competition. It makes no sense for you to target clients who are looking for cheap when you know that you are more expensive. It makes more sense to spend the time to find customers who are more likely to have a long and profitable relationship than look for poor fits; i.e. bad credit risks.

You should know the unique advantages of all of your financial products and be prepared to sell their value to people in industries willing to pay a premium for the highest level of customer care.

You can only convince others of the value of what you are selling when you are convinced of its value. As salespeople, our task is not to impart value to products that have none or even to determine the value of a product to the end user. Your task is to convince your prospects that what you are selling has more value than anything else they could ever buy.

You can only do that when you are thoroughly convinced of the value of what it is you are selling. You've got to believe in what you are selling to make your customers believe in what they are buying.

People buy honesty and recognize it when they interpret your product, service and business practices. They will compare you to other leasing companies, banks, finance companies and to all of their other prior experiences; both good and bad.

Most people can see through a liar. And, sometimes even the best, most talented lessees, get taken. Nonetheless, you still have to ask yourself. After what you said or did during the day, can you sleep at night?

Unfortunately, since there are a lot of "bad" leasing companies and "bad" salespeople in the world, a potential client may falsely accuse you of something. Never take it personally. And don't waste more than 15 minutes trying to convince them of your honesty. It is much better to hold your ground, leave professionally, and move on to your next appointment.

During a tough economy, leasing activity slows down to a trickle. Leasing is directly correlated to the market. When the market is good, leasing is good. When the market is bad, leasing is bad. Unfortunately, if you have mortgaged your life, you still have to bring in the business. And, all too often, some good people tend to start doing bad things, like bringing in the wrong business.

Experience says that you can't focus on winners if you are spending too much time with losers. In fact, as bad as things may be, you must be willing to turn down bad business even when it means a big commission.

Here is one rule that you can never violate:

Do not make false claims for your products, services, or business practices. No amount of glossing over or looking the other way will convince a potential client that your product has value if you know, in your heart and mind, that you cannot deliver what you promise.

Your personal reputation is one of your most valuable assets. You owe it to yourself and your own career to be able to assure your clients of a quality product or service. You don't have to work for anybody who knowingly misleads customers. There are far too many honest and upright leasing companies looking for good salespeople for you to squander your reputation on the few who operate unethically.

In a tough market, you just have to sift through more leads to find the nuggets. Try to keep your perspective. Look at the total size of the leasing market and figure out how much business you have to bring in to be successful. You may be surprised!

Prospecting is a necessary part of sales and something that many sales people do poorly. Done correctly, it becomes as much a part of your routine and as important as a great presentation or a winning close.

And, please remember these helpful hints:

- *Define the type of prospect who is likely to want your offer*
- *Prioritize and work your best prospects*
- *Minimize distractions*
- *Be prepared for the unexpected*
- *Know the common objections and your responses*
- *Review your work at the end of the day*

Use the telephone

People feel comfortable on the telephone. If they have an office they can shut the door. If they have an assistant, they can hold other calls. I find that the best time to call is very early in the morning (before crises begin) or late in the day (when crises are either solved or put on the back burner for another time).

I hate cold calling and love warm calling. I use warm calling to follow up on a letter/e-mail. I feel that I already know the person and, therefore, am not interrupting them.

I picture a telephone conversation as being a pilot trying to land a jumbo jet. Although lessees will try to throw you off your visual runway, it is extremely important to guide yourself during the conversation. Even if you go a little bit off course, your focus should bring you back to center. And, like an airplane that is trying to land, it doesn't matter whether you are a little bit left or right of center, as long as you land on the pavement.

Conversations can make you stand out in a crowd. I have met thousands of leasing professionals at industry events, trade shows, conferences, seminars and conventions over the years. The most successful professionals use their voices effectively.

Top sales professionals distinguish themselves from the rest of the pack by being positive. In today's highly competitive environment, lessees will only give you a chance if they believe that they will not lose anything as a result of starting a relationship with you.

One of the key concepts that I talk about in the classroom is question-answer symmetry. If you ask a good question, you will usually get a good answer. Ask a great question and you will usually get a great answer. To stand out in a crowd, you have to develop great questions and answers.

Before your next telephone call, be prepared to say something that will get the prospect to say to themselves:

- *Do I want to meet this person?*
- *Can this person help me?*
- *Can I afford to take the time away from my other pressing obligations?*
- *What have I got to lose?*
- *Can I pull the plug at any given time?*
- *Will I lose control?*

Dazzle Them With Facts

Once you get the appointment, you need to arrive on time. Your client's time is precious and it is a privilege that they grant time to see you. Always leave extra time between appointments since some customers love to talk. Communication and written skills are essential. Verbal ideas, thoughts and actions ultimately need to be put in writing.

You can also stand out from the crowd by demonstrating integrity on a consistent basis. Never give a lessee an opportunity to question you by giving them inconsistent facts or opinions. Show your flexibility by thinking quickly, adapting accordingly, and offering new alternatives. Do not be afraid to share ideas with a potential lessee. Sometimes, they will check you out before they will work with you.

A good opener increases your probability of success since your audience starts to listen to you, puts their other worries behind them, and awakens them to possibilities previously unimagined. A good opener leverages your speaking skills with visionary support and emotional enlightenment. If you are using a PowerPoint presentation, keep it simple with slow but majestic fade-ins or wipe-outs. You want the audience to focus on the content and not on the effects.

Never spend more than three minutes on any concept. Let your audience talk to you. Listen to their concerns. Most of them will throw preliminary objections at you. Handle them right on the spot.

Write Better Letters

I read every letter and e-mail that I receive, even though I know that 80-90 percent is junk. Why? As a professional educator, I find a lot of my ideas through people who pitch me services.

Experience tells me that you have to establish credibility first. Unless, you give me a convincing argument to proceed, I will read the first 100 words and never read the rest of the message.

If I see a Dear Sir or Occupant or Leasing Professional as an opener, I get angry. I know you took the time and effort to buy my street or e-mail address but did not spend the time or effort to cross-coordinate the information to my name. Why should I trust you? You took a short-cut.

Here are the five basic parts of a good pitch letter.

- ***Use Attention Grabbing Headlines*** - *a great headline is your best opportunity to capture your prospect's attention. Use your headline to immediately tell your prospective customer the number one benefit that she will gain from your product.*
- ***Focus on the Benefits*** - *Benefits tell your customers what they will receive from your product. Reveal 2-3 major benefits so customers will be anxious to meet with you right away. Offer benefits that give you the edge over your competition. In today's market, lessees want a reasonable monthly payment, flexible end-of-term options, easy upgrades and early termination clauses.*
- ***Use Testimonials to Add Credibility*** - *Nothing adds more credibility to your sales letter than testimonials. A testimonial is the equivalent of a trusted friend or respected expert recommending your product. Testimonials help customers feel at ease because testimonials are proof that others have tried your product and were pleased.*
- ***Give Lessees a Reason to Act Now*** - *Give your potential prospects a compelling reason to act immediately. Do you want customers to call now for a free estimate or for special pricing? Determine what immediate action you want customers to take and state clearly how they can take that immediate action.*
- ***Don't Forget to Use Your Postscript*** - *After the headline, the second most-read part of every sales letter is the PS, or the postscript. This is why it's absolutely crucial that you use a PS on every single sales letter you ever write. Use the PS to summarize your offer, introduce an extra bonus or set a limit for the offer. Be sure that your PS is intriguing enough to get your customer to go back and read your entire sales letter.*

Use short sentences. Long sentences make me think that you are trying to convince me that you are intelligent. Intelligent people put their egos on the shelf.

Maximize the use of action verbs. People love to see things move. Watch TV commercials for ideas. My best examples of movement include pouring a beer, drowning a salad with dressing, putting dish washer detergent in a machine, and kids falling into soft pillows. You need to animate your letter and give it life.

Avoid the passive voice. Do not use words like am, be, is, are, etc.

Avoid gerunds. Do not use any word that ends in "ing". Walk, talk, speak has more power than walking, talking, speaking.

You cannot sell leasing on price and stay in this business forever. The best sales people sell leasing on the inherent benefits of leasing.

Reinforce concepts and repeat major ideas. Experts say that you need to state an idea and reinforce the idea at least six times before the listener fully understands what you are saying. Repetition is necessary. However, if you repeat yourself too much you can easily become obnoxious, lose momentum and blow the sale.

Call for action. Too many salespeople give great speeches and then leave lessees, failing to establish the next steps: set up another meeting or agree to a deliverable such as a proposal, contract, or referral. Lessees will not lead themselves to the sale. You need to guide, encourage and direct. If you leave it open, it will stay open.

Follow up at specific times. If you are going to follow up with a potential lessee, you need to establish specific times. Otherwise, you will either not connect or wind up in voice mail hell.

As verbs are to action, adjectives are to descriptions. Use adjectives that describe leasing in a way that will make the lessee feel good about their decision and convince them to proceed. My favorite leasing adjectives include:

- *Appeal*
- *Comfortable*
- *Complete*
- *Convenient*

- *Easy*
- *Exciting*
- *Experienced*
- *Improved*
- *Informative*
- *Money-Saving*
- *New/Advanced*
- *Powerful*
- *Reliable*
- *Results*
- *Service*
- *Superior*

Next time you write a pitch letter, use the preceding checklist to validate the quality of your message. If you are missing any of these items, rewrite the letter and check it again. Remember, you never get a second chance to make a first impression.

Demonstrate Success

You cannot tell people that you are successful. But, you can demonstrate your success by doing things that other successful people do. At first, you may feel awkward and timid. But, as you continue to practice these five rules you will get more comfortable and it will become natural.

- ### Know every aspect of leasing

As I mentioned throughout the book, you need to read as much as you can. Find some time every week to read at least one leasing journal, one leasing newsletter, check out one leasing website and one major newspaper.

In addition, learn as much as you can about the other operations in your company. Acquire as much detail as you can. It is in the details that you will prevent, or at a minimum, minimize mistakes from destroying your relationships.

- **Show a real interest in others**

You cannot fake sincerity. You have to believe it and live it every day. When you put someone else's interest first, they will believe you. And it is through these beliefs that success happens.

Let the other person do most of the talking; be a good listener and stay focused. And, never interrupt.

- **Practice good communication**

If you do not get excited about leasing, then you cannot expect your client/lessee to get excited. Enthusiasm spreads quickly — especially if you have developed trust with your audience. State your points clearly and never rush your presentation.

When I was younger I was asked to speak at a conference. My topic was supposed to last for 1 hour. I finished in 12 minutes. And there was no way for me to recover. The embarrassment lasted weeks and my peers made sure that I remembered.

- **Network all the time**

Networking is the key to success. It is through your network that opportunities will surface. People talk to people all of the time. Of course, your competitors are going to do the same thing. It is the great networker who people think to call when a need or problem arises.

When you network, give them something to remember you by. Offer to help others, especially when it comes to fundraising and not-for-profit activities. Do not be shy about communicating your unique knowledge and expertise to others and share your own personal contacts judiciously.

- ### *Manage stress*

Unless managed, stress will kill you. No ifs, ands or buts. I have seen too many wonderful friends die too soon. And, don't think it cannot happen to you. When you start thinking that way, you start making mistakes, which not only will cost you clients, but may cost you your life.

Compartmentalize worry so that it doesn't carry over from one day to the next. And, ask yourself what is the worst that could happen. Believe me, you need to control your anxiety and it is do-able. But it takes a lot of work.

When business as a whole slows down, it's nothing more than a slump. Many business people say there's little they can do to change the market and they just have to ride it out. The key to finding success within crisis lies in how well you handle what is happening. Succeeding or failing depends upon your attitude — and this is never truer than in challenging times.

In business, the economic climate is always changing. For much of the time, the changes that take place are caused by outside factors that we're powerless to control. But we can control how we react to a situation.

If you are like most successful sales people, you started out your career with an abundance of enthusiasm, desire, excitement and eagerness.

What you have to do in tough times is get back that enthusiasm. There are too many people out there who will tell you no most of your life. During tough times, the number of people who say no rise because you call on more people and more people say no.

The hardest thing to do is keep your focus and remind yourself that this is just a phase that the world is going through. You can't change it. But you can continue to call on people and find those lessees who do need you. Motivating yourself to do what you already know you should do is now your challenge.

Leasing is still as fresh to new clients as it was the day you started — it's just not fresh to you anymore. You've had time not only to see the negatives that every industry, company, and product has, but you've also had time to dwell on them and time to let these negatives affect your actions.

Resolving fears and anxieties is easy when you know how to do it.

I like to use a technique, which I have refined, called the Bubble Meditation. I found that I had to accelerate the process, because the original technique, dating back thousands of years, took too long for me. And, as a result, my anxiety increased instead of decreased.

In order to practice this technique, I will leave a room when I feel anxious. If it is a client meeting, I will ask for a break. If it is in the classroom, I will call for a break. If it is during lunch, I will finish early and go someplace that I feel safe in order to meditate. My two favorite places are bathrooms (usually nearby) and my hotel room or rental car.

You must close your eyes and create a world of silence. Observe your thoughts as they arise spontaneously and naturally. Don't resist them. Imagine that each thought is enclosed in a bubble. Do not worry about how many bubbles you create.

When I first started this meditation, I would create hundreds of bubbles, one for every problem that I thought I had. As I progressed, the number of bubbles began to decline.

Second, picture the color of each bubble and its size. Color usually reflects an emotion. Black represents all emotions while white represents no emotion. Large bubbles represent big problems, while small bubbles represent tiny nuisances.

Then line up all of the bubbles. Do not worry about the time. Time is passing slowly but your mind will race. Although, I do not recommend it, look at your watch. Otherwise, you will create some more anxiety.

Now, let the first bubble (the largest and darkest) float upward as you let go. I like to picture myself at the bottom of a pool of water and watch the sun burst the bubbles as they leave the surface.

After a while in this meditation, you will discover that you have become the observer of your life as well as the subject of your observation.

Many people tell me that they feel lighter after the meditation. I see things clearer, sharper and brighter.

Learn everything you can about Neuro-Linguistic Programming (NLP)

Very few books have changed my life. One of them, written by Anthony Robbins, is called Unlimited Power. The other is How to Master the Art of Selling by Tom Hopkins.

Tony's book introduced me to a new concept called Neuro-Linguistic Programming (NLP), or the science of how the brain works.

Basically, Tony said that one could model human excellence and, therefore, follow the traits of people we want to emulate. In fact, he also said that we could change our lives immediately and develop the skills necessary to become successful.

I try to use his techniques whenever possible. I have used his if/then clues for watching what lessees say and ask and have also used his mirroring techniques in body language role-playing.

So much of rapport-building takes place on a subconscious level. In looking at rapport, there are certain things you can say or do that will win over people. Experts tell us that only 7 percent of communication is in the words we use, 38 percent of communication is in how we say the words we use and the remaining 55 percent of communication is non-verbal.

In understanding non-verbal communication, you must understand how people receive information. This is accomplished through sight, hearing, smell and touch— four of the five senses. Your brain allows you to filter only the data that you want to use at that moment.

Most people tend to favor one of their senses. For example, visual people are typically very good with visual directions. An auditory person prefers to talk in concepts rather than having someone "shoving" a lot of papers in front of him. The kinesthetic person must get a feel about an idea and must be comfortable doing business with you. You can be more effective if you give information to a person in a way that he or she likes to receive it.

People's personalities are often revealed by the words they use. For example, a visual may say, "How does that look to you?" or "Is that clear?" while an auditory may say, "How does that sound?" or "Does that ring a bell?" A kinesthetic may say "Are you comfortable with that?"

Tom, on the other hand, is a master at using body language. He knows that we are judged in the first 15-20 seconds of meeting someone and that there is never a second chance for a good first impression. People judge you, first, audibly when you speak and then they look at you visually and start making judgments. Therefore, you want to be sure you do everything in your power to relax people and cause them to want to be with you.

When people are like each other, they tend to like each other. This concept can be particularly powerful in matching the "tone", "tempo" and "posture" of the prospect.

Other techniques that Tom encourages include smiling, looking people in the eyes (Tony calls this looking into one's soul), remembering people's names, and using handshakes.

Steer the Conversation

Successful leasing professionals never give anyone the impression that they're pushing them - for the simple reason that they never push. But they do lead the prospect from the initial contact to happy involvement in signing the contract.

Have you ever been surprised at how freely you've talked to certain salespeople before buying from them? They were alert and interested. You felt comfortable with them . Recalling those conversations, you may think you were leading and the salesperson was following. Superficially, that was true - at first. In a deeper sense, however, that professional salesperson was leading all the way and you were following his direction.

How did that happen? He encouraged you by asking you a great question or for permission to proceed. In either case, you believed that you were in control. Once he set the direction, he slowly began to lead you on one or more paths to a closing.

Negotiation tactics

Keep a couple of 'goodies' in your pocket. Never give away your final offer up-front. You have no room no maneuver. Focus your efforts on the crux of the problem. There are only one-two major objections that stall a deal. All the others are minor and can be fixed.

Make as few promises as possible. Never promise something that you cannot deliver. People remember promises and remember when you fail to deliver. It is better to call and apologize in advance than pretend that you are an ostrich with your head in the sand.

Anticipate potential customer objections. Learn how to answer the major objections with skill and grace until doing so becomes natural and professional.

Be aware of the Teflon statement

Sometimes, people do not like to tell you to stop. Yet they give you signals that basically say that they want the conversation to end. I call these Teflon statements, since they do not want anything to 'stick' to them.

I have found it nearly impossible to respond to a Teflon statement without making things worse. My best example is when Toby, my wife, says to me, "You do not understand". I know that there is absolutely nothing that I can say that will not make things worse.

For example, if I say I do understand, I am disagreeing with her observation. If I say you don't understand me, I am fueling the fire.

Here are other examples that lessees have said to me, "You don't understand my business", "I am unique", "We've always done it that way", "I already have a leasing company, "I'm just gathering information for my boss", and "I cannot tell one leasing company from another" and "all leasing companies are alike."

When I hear a Teflon statement I try to reschedule the meeting for a better time.

Handling Objections

My research indicates that leasing elicits only 14 major objections. Here are some of the most common objections that you will hear:

- *We always pay cash. (Great — all of my clients pay cash — they just pay me monthly)*
- *Your rates are too high. (Compared to what?)*
- *I am more comfortable with a loan. (May I show you our better-than-loan loan? It is called a finance lease).*
- *I got burnt by another leasing company. (I'm sorry to hear that. Would you mind sharing with me what happened so that we can make sure that it does not happen again?)*
- *I want to be able to cancel at will. (If we put that feature into our lease are you prepared to sign today?)*
- *I don't want to make a down payment. (Several of our lease programs do not require down payments — may I show you one of them?)*
- *We cannot get out of our existing lease — (If I can show you how to do that are your ready to sign today?)*

A great objection that you will often hear is "What makes your company unique?" What they are basically asking is:

"How do you create a perceived value to differentiate yourself from the competition when you are both selling a commodity?"

That objection comes up a lot in leasing. Especially, since most people think leasing is just about money. And it is very hard to distinguish one type of money from another.

So, what do you do? Simply detail and communicate the important ways you are different from your competitors.

Even if your price is identical, you can always find a unique way to differentiate yourself in the marketplace. Your financial product may be identical, but everything else about your program may be different. For example, let's say your potential lessee is considering you and another company. Sometimes, you want to compare yourself on size (they're small, you're global or they're global and you're local) and experience (they're old, you're new, they're new, you're experienced)

Differentiating Your Product

Think about everything that is associated with leasing — pricing, documentation, structure, end-of-term options, residual position, and tax position. Create several categories, and label columns on a piece of paper with the names of each category.

Now, consider each column one at a time, and list all the ways that your lease differs from your competitor's in that column.

Then, pick out those differences that are most important to your prospect. Keep in mind that what you see as important may not be viewed that way by your potential lessee or vendor. Take the time to critically analyze your list and eliminate those items that are not important to your customer, items that don't impact their jobs or make a difference to them.

Finally, translate each of the remaining items (I recommend only three) into statements of benefit to the customer.

Now that you've professionally prepared, you are ready to communicate those differences to your customer. You need to point them out in an organized and persuasive presentation.

Prepare a sell sheet with each of the differences noted as a bullet. Next to each bullet, write a few comments that summarize the benefit statements you prepared. Then, meet with your customer, lay the sheet down in front of her, and walk through *it, explaining each point as you go.*

Treat it like you would any other well-done presentation. Be sensitive to your customer's reaction, and ask for feedback as you talk through the list. Say, "How does that sound?" or "Does that make sense to you?" and emphasize those things that seem to be more important to your customer. Then, leave that sheet with your customer.

I'm always amazed at the number of salespeople who are confounded by the customer's perception that their product is just like the other guy's, when those salespeople have done nothing to demonstrate the differences to the potential lessee.

If you have done a good job of analyzing, preparing, and communicating, your customer's perception should be altered, and you gain the business. If you haven't done well at this, then your customer will continue to see no difference between buying it from you and buying from the next guy. And, if you haven't shown him sufficient reason to buy it from you, then he shouldn't.

Follow these rules and you will see few of your customers treating you like a commodity.

Sample Closes

Closing a leasing sale is by far the most important step in the selling process. If you don't love it now, learn to love it, because that's where the money is.

When you first start out selling anything, there is a natural inclination to not ask for the sale. We spend a lot of time prospecting, finding potential clients, making wonderful presentations and then, for some reason, we avoid asking for the sale.

Psychologists would argue that asking somebody for something is intimidating and that it is much easier to avoid asking. However, you can go broke very quickly.

Dad used to say to me, "What would you say to a homeless man, sitting on the street, with only $1 in his tin cup that would get him to part with all or part of his *money?" He then would tell me that you have to find a bona fide, honest reason to show him how he would benefit by giving up something. Often, I would see Dad convince the guy and reward him with a $10 bill.*

Initially, as a kid, I thought Dad was cruel. But, on the other hand, I never knew how he changed the poor man's belief in himself and others. In hindsight, I can see how Dad gave poor strangers enough ability to trust him.

The best salespeople acquire an instinct which gives them the ability to go for the close all the time. They constantly try test closes and go into the final closing sequence when they think it is the right time. Yes, it is a gift. But it can be learned.

Too many salespeople get wrapped up in their selling sequence and lose track of the customer. Believe it or not, there are clients out there who will get sold fast. However, if you keep talking instead of closing, you run the risk of un-selling them.

To become a top sales professional, you must always have your closing materials with you and be ready to close anywhere and at any time. I've always argued that the best leasing professionals can read signals, adapt quickly, and improvise. It also happens to be what makes a great actor!

In watching students in class and professionals out in the field, I am amazed that many avoid closing. In questioning them, they tell me that they are afraid of being pushy or getting the client to buy something that they do not want.

Let me remind you, that as a salesperson, it is your responsibility to lead your client to a decision that will make their life better. If you do not attempt to close, then you are doing a disservice to your client.

Here are some of my favorites:

- ### Try it you'll like it

Position the transaction as a small deal. For example, what have you got to lose? We're only talking $100,000 compared to $10,000,000 in financing that you *awarded so far this year.*

- **Specials (Preferred)**

Susan, we can only offer this rate to you because of your excellent credit rating.

- **Double binds**

The double bind close effectively uses the word 'or' to create a perception of choice. Would you prefer the $1 out or the 10 percent balloon option? Would you like to close at the end of this month or at the beginning of next month?

- **Permission**

Similar to the double bind close, this technique effectively uses the word "if". If we incorporate "a cancel at will" option, will you sign today?

- **Imagination**

This technique fast forwards to the future and puts you in the lessee's vision. Sir, at the end of this three year contract, I want to be able to sit down with you and have you tell me what made this transaction work.

- **Similar product**

You are correct. Our product is similar to others in the marketplace. But, may I should you the unique differences in our contract and service that distinguish us in the marketplace?

Welcome to the Leasing Industry
Next Chapter: Quit Complaining

Chapter 13

QUIT COMPLAINING

Toby, my wife, grew up in Brooklyn. She raised two children on her own and struggled to make end's meet. Although money was extremely tight, she always found the money to send her children to summer camp and she made sure that they had food on the table every night. She was able to save enough money to send them to college and took a vacation once every 7-10 years. She never once complained about her situation.

I've learned a lot from Toby. She has brought to me a whole new perspective that I have never had before. Growing up in Brooklyn is different from the rest of the world. She has a unique set of expressions that amaze me. She will respond to my thoughts even before I've had a chance to finish what I am saying. She seems to know what I am thinking all the time.

If I complain about my day and I expect a little sympathy, she says, What is your problem?" or "What's the matter with you?" It is hard to describe her voice, but it comes across in a very sarcastic way. At first, I was not used to someone talking to me in that fashion. But after fourteen years it has had a major positive effect on me.

When I get to feel sorry for myself and I hear her, I feel different. I realize that I am complaining about something fairly trivial compared to what she had gone through and that I'd better get back on track real fast and deal with the problem.

My grandparents grew up in Europe and survived World War II. Although they never were in concentration camps, they knew many people who were. People tell me that concentration camp survivors are happy to be alive and that they rarely complain about anything. They know the alternative.

I have personally traveled to and worked in Nigeria. The tragedy there cannot be believed. The pot-holed streets are full of trash and the 100-degree days create smoke-filled hues in the crowded flea markets. Twelve-year-old children prostitute their bodies to anyone who has the money, and elderly people mob cars as they attempt to sell fruit and bread to survive. When I see their faces, I am reminded that I have nothing to complain about.

I have two children. Jordana goes to school at Wake Forest in Raleigh, North Carolina. Moira lives with my ex-wife in a small town called Oriental, North Carolina. The town has 600-1000 residents (depending upon the season), 2-3 schools for different levels of education, 1 traffic light, 1 grocery store and a post office. For many years the town lacked basics such as cable television, ATM's and fast food restaurants. Because my children lived there since they were babies, they never complained because they never experienced what they were missing.

Problems at Work

Try this on for size. If you complain about too few clients, think about the time when you will have too many clients to handle. If you complain about too little cash, think about the time when the banks are going to fall over themselves wooing your business. Focus your efforts on getting more revenue instead of complaining. Focus on prospects, call on former clients, talk to your networking sources, take on part time jobs, talk to recruiters, talk to government agencies and do something positive.

If you have problems with staff turnover, think about the time when you will have to turn down prospective employees. Turn to the newspapers, friends, networking partners. They will help you find staff.

You have no right to complain — you can change

Think back to why you wanted to go into sales. It does not matter whether you were downsized or decided to leave on your own. Your position can be changed. Complaining will not do a thing for you nor solve the problem.

I am sure that when you decided to go into leasing you felt like you were on a honeymoon; that everything was perfect and that there was no stopping you. Unfortunately, fate may have played you a dirty trick. Being entrepreneurial brings tremendous advantages along with the disadvantages that you will feel from time to time.

Complaining about a problem does not solve it. You must deal with the problem head on and work on it until it goes away. Yes, other problems will come, but you will deal with those, too.

How to stop complaining

Here is a very simple process that will break your habit of complaining. Take a deep breath. Find a mirror. Force a smile on your face and ask yourself the following two questions:

- Who has a worse problem?

- Would I want to be that person right now?

There will always be someone out there who is worse off than you. Remember that fact, and get back on track so that you can deal with your problem. If you are the type of person who gets angry, take a pillow and hit it against the bed. Get rid of your negative emotions and focus on solving the problem that is causing you to complain.

If you need time to think, do something while you are thinking. Take your mind off the problem. Take five minutes and do something positive. Read a book. Watch television. Go outside. Do something constructive. Build something. Compose a poem. Write an article. Get lost in the woods. Get yourself an ice cream cone.

Yell, scream and get angry

Every chapter your have read so far in this book has told you to act responsibly, professionally and courteously to your piers, mentors, customers, family, associates and everyone else you work with in your business.

Nonetheless, there will be times when you will feel the need to explode, the need to let go and really blast people who have taken advantage of your kind nature.

Who are these people? It's impossible to identify them up front because you can never know who they are. But, when it happens, you will know it. It can come in the form of a colleague who steals your ideas and creates a competing business, an associate who gives your trade secrets to a competitor, a young employee who takes supplies from the inventory cabinet, a lawyer who fails to perform adequately in protecting your interests, a real estate agent who blows a major sale, an accountant who appears to know his stuff and doesn't, a former employee who tells the world about your personal life or a reporter who twists your story to make headlines.

There are many people out there who will attempt to hurt you in your endeavors to grow your business. Most of the time, their actions are not illegal and are just immoral and unethical. And, I know of no country or society that has successfully protected people against immoral and unethical behavior.

So what can you do? I suggest that you yell, scream and get angry. By doing this, you will feel better and provide yourself with the ammunition to go on to better opportunities. I do not suggest that you act this way all the time nor yell at people for insignificant misdemeanors. I simply state that a good yell can make your innermost feelings more secure. And by doing so, you will be able to get back on track as quickly as possible.

In addition to yelling try these alternative methods for regaining your momentum:

Take a pillow and hit a wall

I have found that slamming a pillow against a wall does several things. It not only lets my anger out, it lets the laughter in. After a few seconds of slamming a pillow, I feel exhilarated at the positive feeling and begin to laugh at the absurdity of the situation. By using a pillow, I am not damaging anything in my office. If you keep your anger inside of you to the end of the day, you will do damage to your blood pressure and your heart. And you do not want to die in building a business. It's not worth it.

Pretend to sue your assailant

Although it is impractical to sue a person for immoral and unethical behavior, it is nice to know that you can fake out your mind with biased role playing. By pretending to sue your assailant, you can visualize success in the court of your mind. Since you control the court, you control the outcome. By giving yourself this needed victory, you will feel more empowered to take on the real tasks of the day and accomplish positive things.

Get even

When someone has hurt me in the past, I looked at ways to get even. Getting even is very easy. Let other people know what happened. Do it in an appropriate way since you do not want legal action for slander to be brought against you. Inform your assailant's boss, suppliers, and neighbors. Use facts and do not embellish about the emotional aspects. You are simply providing information to another professional because you do not want them to get hurt like you did. The irony is, you receive a lot more business as a result of using your bad experience to protect others.

Make a list

I have kept a list of people who have hurt me over the years and I never share it with anyone, except Toby. It is personal and I like it that way. It keeps me focused on how small the number of incidents have been over my twenty plus years in the training business. Surprisingly, the list continues to grow and statistically the number of people who get added each year is a constant percentage. Therefore, no matter how smart you get, how wise you think you are, nature has a way of spreading bad things to all people.

What I have found amazing is that I look back at some of the names and smile. I smile because I learned something in every incident - that I would go on and that I would become more successful in my life.

Chapter 14

THANK GOD

Sales professionals love to take chances. They jump into situations based on their gut feeling and believe that they cannot fail. They respond quickly without having the luxury to think about potential problems. Often, the facts would tell them to stop.

They are like stunt men, artists, writers, composers, and architects. All of these people have something in common. They are the first to create products, programs, or acts which have never been done before. And like their artistic counterparts, salespeople become successful based upon society's acceptance of their unique ideas and products.

Although many salespeople fail, many rise to the top of their field. Most of the successful salespeople have failed once or twice before they found the winning formula. Examples of failed entrepreneurs who ultimately made it include Walt Disney, Henry Ford, Thomas Edison and Colonel Saunders. They made it through hard work, persistence, timing and luck.

Successful sales professionals need to believe in fate. Whether you believe in God, or some spiritual leader, it is practically impossible to succeed without some form of luck. Luck usually comes to you in the form of being in the right place at the right time. That right time could be in the form of making the right phone call, going to the right meeting, or writing the right proposal. Although you can increase your odds by making more phone calls, going to more meetings, and writing more proposals, your fate is still in the hands of some unknown force; a factor which we cannot control.

Start talking to God if you have not started

It does not matter if you have never believed in God before. I only started believing in God when my first business was failing. I kept asking myself what did I do wrong and what was going to happen to me? Who was I talking to when I asked those questions? Whether I was talking to another person, a spiritual concept or my internal self, I still needed to ask for guidance and assistance. As a sales professional, you will need to talk to a higher power that can help you. God does not care if you are asking for assistance for the first time in your life. All that matters is that you are asking.

God helps those who help themselves. By reading this book, you've already made another step toward a better life. And, like pioneers and immigrants, you want to get a greater slice of life.

You need to believe that God would never want you to fail, but you may fail several times before you achieve success.

You may need to fail before you succeed

Although there are many circumstances where people succeed the first time, there are more stories of failed sales professionals. Failure is not bad. You are still alive and have the opportunity to start all over again. Tom Watson, who ran IBM for many years, called a young man into his office after hearing that he spent $6 million dollars on a project that yielded no results. The young man went into Watson's office and brought with him his resignation. Watson looked at the man and said, Why would I want to fire you after I've just invested $6 million in your education? Go back, learn from your experience and try again.

In a way, one can thank God for failures because it is the price one has to pay to achieve success. As long as you have the opportunity to try again, all you have lost is time, money and friends. And as much as this may hurt, you still have more time on this planet to live a better life, more opportunity and wisdom to earn more money than you lost and new friends who will come along as a result of you hanging around a different set of people who have shared the same experiences that you have.

Thank God for clues and dreams

When something happens that doesn't seem to make sense, ask yourself if God is attempting to get your attention. God has a strange sense of humor. There will be days when nothing will go right. There will be times that you cannot believe that this is happening to you. There will be moments when you feel an energy running through your body as you see something for the first time. There will be times when you achieve something that you did not expect, like a new client, a found parking space, a great restaurant, a new view from a mountain. Listen carefully to your inner thoughts and use them to guide you. Clues will help you figure things out.

My favorite God story goes as follows:

An unexpected flood came to town. All of the residents were fleeing except one man who decided to take out a ladder and climb up to the roof of his home. As people were running out of town, they yelled up to him and told him to get out of town or he would die. He sat there calmly and said, "Don't worry. God will take care of me."

As the floods continued to rise, people would come by in their rowboats. They told him that he was going to die if he stayed and that he should leave his home immediately and come with them. Again, he calmly said, "Don't worry. God will take care of me."

Finally, as the flood is about to reach the roof line, a helicopter flies over, drops a rope, and tells him he has to abandon his home. Once again, without missing a heartbeat, he says, "God will take of me."

Of course, the floods rise and he dies. As he enters Heaven, he sees God and tells him that God abandoned him in his hour of need. God calmly responded, "How many signals do I have to send you?"

Chapter 15

SUCCESS COMES IN MANY PACKAGES

Pretend you are successful until you are successful.

Most sales professionals have difficulty defining success. Some define it externally. They use their acquisitions, like cars, homes, jewelry and lifestyle to signify their worth to themselves and their community. Others define it internally. They have a peace of mind and are so quiet that you would never know that they are successful.

On the way to success, you will stumble many times. Think about riding on a wild horse and falling off. Basically, you have two choices; stay on the ground or get back on the horse. Believe me, when you are lying on the ground and smarting, your first reaction is to stay on the ground.

If you do not get back on the horse, you are not going to go anywhere and you will feel unsuccessful. It is at these times that you need to pretend that you have already been able to get back on the horse thousands of times. You need to feel that feeling and get back on the horse without a second's notice. Do that often enough and you will get back on the horse without hesitation.

Success is a feeling. A feeling is something that cannot be denied by you or another person. You own your feelings and your decisions. If you decide to stay on the ground, that is your decision. That does not mean that it is a bad decision. It only means that you may not get to where you want to be. And, you need the horse to get you there! So you'd better get back on the horse.

Strugglers feel that they fail along the way. They cut back on their lifestyle. They remove themselves from the rest of the world. They isolate themselves from their friends and loved ones. They stop going places and focus on money. They worry about where their next cash flow is coming from. It is OK to worry but not to the point that it distracts you.

Pretending to be successful requires you to focus on a different definition of success. Focus on the smallest detail as if you were focusing on the efforts of a baby starting out in the world. If a baby stands up and falls down, do not focus on the fact that the baby fell down. Focus on the fact that the baby attempted to stand up.

Success is in your mind and not anyone else's. So you need to surround yourself with reminders that you are already successful:

- *You took a chance*
- *You are willing to risk your future on an idea*
- *You are willing to proceed even if everyone else thinks it is a bad idea*
- *Your credit cards will support you in the short term*
- *You are in good health*
- *You love getting up in the morning*
- *You control your life*
- *You have unlimited opportunity*
- *You can change*
- *You can give to others*
- *You can start over again each and every day*
- *You love yourself*
- *You get advice from others*
- *You are going to make it*

Pretend you are successful until you become successful and you will soon realize that you are already there. On that note, welcome to the best world that I know — the world of equipment leasing.